MW01256917

THE PALM SUNDAY TORNADO

A Novel by

TIMOTHY BONTRAGER

Based on the events of April 11, 1965

This book is the work of fiction. Names, characters, places, and incidents are the product of the author's imagination or are used fictitiously.

If you purchase this book without a cover you should be aware that this book may have been stolen property and should be reported as "unsold and destroyed" to the author. In such case the author has not received any payment for this "stripped book."

Copyright 2005 by Timothy Bontrager
All rights reserved. No part of this book may be reproduced in any form, by any electronic or mechanical means, including information storage and retrieval systems, without permission in writing from the author, except by a reviewer who may quote brief passages in a review.

Cover design by Timothy Bontrager
Cover photo is copyright to The Truth Publishing Company.
Reprinted with permission.

Timothy Bontrager
P.O. Box 377
Middlebury, IN 46540

www.TimothyBontrager.com
Join the Timothy Bontrager eNewsletter.

Second Paperback Printing: April 2006
ISBN 1-59196-964-6

For my parents
Eugene and Barbara

Acknowledgements

This book would not exist without the help of many people. I'd especially like to thank my family, who support me and all of my crazy ideas. I love you all. Sondra, my wife, I'm sorry for all of the nights, mornings, weekends, and spare time it took to complete this book. Thank you and I love you.

I'd like to thank The Truth Publishing Company for allowing me to use the infamous "twin tornado" photo for the cover.

I'd also like to thank my editor, Ryan Miller. Where would this book be without you? Thank you for your guidance and your friendship.

THE PALM
SUNDAY TORNADO

PROLOGUE

Imagine looking out your window to find a tornado one mile wide racing toward you at 60 mph. That's literally what thousands of people saw on April 11, 1965. This story is just as much theirs as it is my dad's.

Nobody ever deserves to go through what my dad did. Everything about his life changed in a matter of seconds. He lost everything. I'm not talking about clothes, or baseball cards, or even a pet, even though he did lose all of those things. I'm talking about never again hearing the sound of a harmonica coming from the front porch or following the scent of a homemade apple pie into the kitchen. My dad lost the two people he never thought he'd be without. At the age of eighteen, he lost his parents, killed by twin tornadoes, one right after the other.

Who do you turn to when you no longer have a father's guidance or a mother's embrace? How do you know what you're supposed to do when you are all alone in this world? Those are questions I've never been able to ask my dad. In all of my twenty-six years of existence we had never once talked about what happened on April 11, 1965. Just two months ago, that finally changed. I used to know April 11th as the day my dad needed to be left alone. Now, I actually know why.

I wish I could change the way things happened, but I know I can't. The sad thing is, I know he's not the only one who distinctly remembers that Palm Sunday. There are many others just like him, who lost everything.

My name is Ethan. The story I'm about to tell you is real. No, I wasn't there when it happened, but I feel like I was. I'll do my best to tell you everything my dad told me.

CHAPTER 1

David Miller slapped his alarm clock as soon as it rattled to life. He knew if he got up it meant sitting through Sunday school and another one of Mr. Yoder's ramblings. Mr. Yoder's hair formed a silver horseshoe around his head. He liked to stretch thin strands from one side to the other.

David was thinking it was time he started making some decisions on his own and cutting church was one of them. He rolled away from the door and nestled under the quilt his mother had made him, when he heard footsteps come pattering down the hallway toward him. He was certain it was his little sister and one of his parents coming to wake him up. The door squeaked as it opened and footsteps slithered toward him until they bumped into his bed.

"David, time to get up," his mother said.

David grinned. He knew his mother couldn't see his face. His plan was to drag out this charade long enough so he wouldn't have time to get ready for Sunday school.

Rebecca, his little sister, tapped him on the shoulder. "Day-vee," she sang. "Day-vee. Time to get up."

It was hard to resist her two-year-old voice, but David didn't budge. He could tell her eyes were on him, waiting for any kind of movement. She giggled to herself as she touched the bottom of his right foot, just out from the blanket covering him. It tickled so much he almost burst. Somehow, he didn't even flinch. The second time, she giggled louder. This time it just made him mad, yet he stayed as stiff as stone.

After a moment, Rebecca and her mother gave up and went to make breakfast.

David took a deep breath. So far so good. His plan was working. The morning sun cast a crisp checkerboard through the cross sections of the window onto his bed. A cluster of sparrows sang as they hopped between budding branches outside his window.

Ten minutes later, the voice he'd been expecting

echoed throughout his room. "David, let's go. Get up." His father sounded like a drill sergeant; deep, clear and to the point. This was the battle.

David squirmed under his covers as though rudely awakened from a deep sleep. He could tell his father wasn't buying it. He felt a shove against his bed.

"David, get up," his father said again. He pushed David on the shoulder.

David rolled toward his father. He squinted and rubbed his eyes. "What?"

"Get up. Get ready for church."

David looked his father square in the eyes. "I'm not going."

His father wasted no time. He yanked the covers down, grabbed David's arm and pulled him out of bed. He stood him up directly in front of him and pointed toward his closet. "Now get ready for church."

David jerked his arm out of his father's right-handed grip. He felt a surge of energy race through his veins. "Church is boring, and besides, I'm eighteen now and I don't want to go. So, I'm not going."

David's father glared back at him, his fists clenched. David sucked in his breath. He hadn't anticipated this.

"You're going because I said so." David's father clenched his jaw. "I expect you to be ready in fifteen minutes."

David took a small step backward.

His father looked out the window, then took a deep breath. "Today is Palm Sunday. You obviously don't know what that means." He turned his back from David, shaking his head. "It's one of the worst Sundays you could have tried to skip."

And that was that.

David went to church, sat through Sunday school, and doodled another caricature that resembled Mr. Yoder. There were nearly one hundred people at the service, all sitting on hardwood benches. The preacher stood behind a homemade wooden pulpit as his message carried out of two speakers. Men sported their best three-piece suits while women wore their newest spring dresses.

In retaliation for David's morning tirade, his father invited Mr. Yoder and his wife over for lunch. The last time they were over, David had to sit through two hours of Mr. Yoder's stories. Every time David had tried to get up, his father made him sit back down. Today was no different.

"Good dinner, wasn't it?" David's father asked, after Mr. Yoder and his wife finally left. He was seated in a wicker rocking chair he'd made himself. He'd been writing in his journal, pausing only to look out the living room window.

David hadn't spoken to his father since their confrontation. He'd managed little conversation at the dinner table too, but it was time; time to have it out with his father.

David sat up on the black and gray cross-stitched couch and leaned toward his father. "I can't believe you invited them over for dinner."

His father's head jolted toward him. He pulled off his reading glasses. "Excuse me?"

David turned off the radio next to him on the floor. "You heard me."

David's father clasped shut his journal and placed it on the end table beside him. He set his glasses on top of his journal as he stood up. "You've got quite the mouth."

David gritted his teeth hard enough to make a vein bulge in his forehead. He was a man now. He should be treated like one. That's all he wanted.

David inched his way to the edge of the couch. He was ready to jump at his father if he needed to. "I don't know what your problem is, but you know I can't stand going to Sunday school, let alone church. What's the big deal if I don't go anymore?"

David's father stood in front of him looking down. His shoulders were broad, his chest thick from years of farm work, and his hands were tough as leather.

"I'll tell you what the big deal is. It's the way you're speaking to your father."

David rose from the couch and stood nose to nose with his father. For the first time, he noticed puffy bags underneath his father's eyes and deep wrinkles spreading from the corners.

Instead of pushing him like he wanted to, David

brushed past his father and walked toward the front door. "I'm sick of being treated like a baby!" He harnessed the adrenaline racing through him and shoved the screen door open.

"Then quit acting like one!" his father yelled back.

The screen door slammed shut.

David jolted awake. He sat up in bed and rubbed his eyes. Another dream, just like all the others.

A rumble of clouds smashed together outside. A blast of lightning followed, illuminating the room. His wife, Jeanne, was lying next to him. He had thrown his pillow and the blankets to the floor.

David climbed out of bed and tiptoed over to watch the rain splatter against the windowpane. He leaned his elbow on the ledge and dropped his head to his hand.

His wife rustled and let out a deep breath. "Honey, are you okay?" she asked.

Ignoring her question, he pulled the drapes shut, rearranged the blankets, and crawled back into bed.

"Are you okay?" she asked again.

David lifted his left arm, inviting her to snuggle against his chest.

"Just go back to sleep. I'm fine."

CHAPTER 2

The following morning, David and his wife, Jeanne, sat in the living room in the dark. As typical, neither of them said a word. They took turns breaking the silence with coffee slurps. Years of practice had taught them how to ease into each day.

Nothing had been mentioned about the storm last night or David's dream. Jeanne knew better than to initiate the conversation, like she wanted to. David wasn't much of a talker in the morning. He always joked that he liked to keep his mind from thinking until it absolutely had to. If David wanted to talk about his dream, then he'd bring it up.

Jeanne was left with the warmth of her mug to calm
her worries.

With her brown eyes and soft skin
complimented by her highlighted brown hair, Jeanne
was always thought of as lovely. Though no one
understood why, she constantly hopped on and off
diets, always trying the latest fad. She loved to
cook, keep her house clean, and entertain guests.
She took the most pride in taking care of her
husband. She often surprised him with a
handwritten note, hidden where only he'd find it.
Her favorite time with David was when they'd take
long walks across their property, holding hands. It
was obvious, she loved him deeply. However, the
most frustrating part of their marriage was what was
happening right now.

For nearly forty years, David has possessed his
own built-in seasonal system. The dreams always
come back with the first thunderstorm of the spring.
David saw two counselors, took three different
medications, and even visited a dream interpreter.
They all told him the same thing: he carried grief,
regret, and guilt. They each reiterated the same
remedy too. He did nothing wrong and needs to find
a way to reconcile with himself. He has tried, Lord
knows he has tried, but apparently he doesn't know
what that means or how to do it.

Jeanne lowered her mug. "Good morning," she
said.

Ethan, their son, simply nodded his pillow-matted hair in their direction. After pouring a cup of coffee, Ethan found himself in what had become his usual spot in the living room, the dark blue recliner. He propped his feet up, leaned back, and held the warm mug against his stomach.

After a few more minutes of silence, David stood up, kissed Jeanne on the forehead, and loafed toward the kitchen. Ethan witnessed this almost every morning.

For some reason, Ethan could tell his mom was sorely disappointed this morning. He watched her head track David as he walked past the glass end table, the grandfather clock, and then the china cabinet. David turned on the light above the kitchen stove and placed his coffee mug in the dishwasher. He paused to inspect a new crack in the wall just below the ceiling. He ran his fingers over it seeming to ponder how such a thing was possible. Nonetheless, he turned off the light as he left the kitchen.

Jeanne crossed her legs and shook her head from side to side. Then, she shifted her gaze to the front window.

"Did you sleep okay?" she asked.

Ethan groaned. "Uh huh."

Jeanne slurped her coffee, then let out a breath. "Did you hear the storm last night?"

"Yeah." Ethan rolled his head and groaned again. "I watched it."

Jeanne turned toward Ethan. "You did?"

Ethan sniffed, then sighed. "Yep. From the porch."

Ethan grew up in a white, two-story, colonial house. There were two bedrooms and a storage room upstairs, an open living room, dining room and kitchen, all with wooden floors, downstairs. A porch wrapped around the front and side of the house where a porch swing hung by chains. The windows were hard to open, the basement was dark and scary, and the oak trees that lined both sides of the dirt lane were overgrown.

Ethan had discovered years ago that there was a perfect spot on the porch for watching storms. He had a front row seat for the entire production on the wooden-porch swing. It was tucked in beside a brick wall.

"It was some storm wasn't it?" she asked. Jeanne used to take Ethan to the basement every time there was a hard storm. She was terrified of them. Ethan knew she wished he would be scared of them too. Instead, he seemed to rather enjoy the display of power.

"Sure was."

Jeanne set her coffee mug on the end table and began fluffing the pillows on the couch.

"Was dad up last night?" he asked even though he already knew the answer.

Jeanne rolled her eyes, then situated the pillows just right. "Spring is here." That was all she said.

With that simple comment Ethan knew that last

night marked the start of the toughest time of the year. His dad would be distant, short on words, and irritable, even more than normal.

"I guess not much has changed since I've been gone," he said.

CHAPTER 3

The sky changed from pitch black to dark purple as Ethan drove to work. Just two short months ago, he wouldn't have had any idea what that looked like. He simply wouldn't have noticed.

Ethan had been living in Denver, Colorado. He was an engineer in a plastics manufacturing plant with a ten-hour workday. He moved there after graduating from college hoping to hit the slopes and enjoy the city life. Instead, he spent most of his time digging out from underneath a mountainous pile of work. He was handed any project a senior engineer simply didn't want to do. Finally, after four years, and not one single promotion, he decided to quit and move home.

Middlebury, typical of most Midwest small towns, is lined with narrow buildings three stories high, home to businesses and restaurants, all family-owned. Taco Bell, McDonalds, and Dairy Queen are the only restaurant chains in town. The nearest Wal-Mart is a thirty-five minute drive straight west. It's a place where neighbors sit on their porches in their wicker furniture and watch as people pass by. Bed-and-breakfasts, rarely vacant, line Main Street until it turns into State Road 13, a road leading to acres of green pastures and cornfields. Tourists can't seem to get enough of the nearby flea market or some old-fashioned Amish cooking.

As Ethan was getting used to life at home, he often wondered what in the world he was thinking when he decided to move back. He immediately missed the city, having everything he wanted just down the street and people everywhere. At times he even missed his job and the feeling of being important and irreplaceable. And now he carried an underlying feeling of being a failure because he was once again living under his parents' roof. Yet, there was something about the simplicity of this town, of this kind of life, that reassured him he had made the right decision.

Ethan landed a job that required his alarm to go off at 5 a.m., so he began joining his parents in their morning ritual. Somehow, the silence of the early morning helped him feel ready for the day. Hours of random conversations and millions of tedious tasks were waiting for him as soon as he got to work. Yet, those very things were what made his day fly by so quickly.

Ethan worked at One More Cup, a coffee shop in Elkhart, a neighboring town west of Middlebury. One More Cup sits on Colonial Avenue, a historic block of nostalgic buildings built in the 1800s. The green and tan walls stretch to the twenty-foot high ceiling, where dim lights dangle by black cords. Customers lounge on eclectic couches and chairs, clustered throughout the narrow coffee shop.

One More Cup provided him with that little sense of city life he was missing. He loved the atmosphere almost as much as the people he'd met. However, he hated the hours and there was no way to keep track of how many smoothies or cappuccinos he'd made. Nonetheless, Ethan had done very little job searching since he was in no hurry to put on his engineering hat. This job was exactly what he needed even if he was twenty-six years old standing behind the counter at a coffee shop.

"I'll take a large coffee, black, to go. And make it quick, coffee boy."

Ethan recognized that voice without even looking up. It was Johnny, his best friend.

Ethan slanted his head, annoyed. "I'll see what I can do."

They smiled at each other and shook hands.

"How's it going?" asked Johnny.

Ethan grabbed a to-go cup and pushed on the coffee dispenser. "Oh, just fine. How about you?"

"Not bad."

Ethan set the to-go coffee on the counter and rang up the order.

Johnny smirked just loud enough for Ethan to hear.

"What?" asked Ethan.

Johnny shook his head from side to side. "I never thought I'd see this, you serving me coffee at One More Cup."

Ethan rolled his eyes. "I know. Live it up."

Johnny handed Ethan his money. "It's not like you to go from Mr. Engineer to this."

Ethan handed him his change. "Well, I'll take this any day over the crap I was doing."

Johnny nodded. He picked up his coffee and turned to leave, but stopped, catching Ethan's attention. "Hey what do you think about a meeting at the Armory tomorrow night?"

It took a moment for the question to register in Ethan's mind, but when it did he smiled. A meeting at the Armory meant some real, unhindered guy-time, just like during high school and summer breaks of college. This was exactly what he needed.

"Sounds good to me," he said.

After Johnny was gone Ethan couldn't help but smile at what Johnny had said. *"It's not like you."* He was right. Working at the coffee shop wasn't something Ethan would normally do, but that's part of why he liked it. At his engineering job in Denver he had long hours, few friends, and a high level of stress. All he had to do now was make sure he got each person's order right. He actually liked working the early morning and lunch shift because that meant he was free by the afternoon.

He really enjoyed all of the different people he saw on a regular basis. Most of the police force came in each morning because they only had to pay half price for their coffee, so he knew them on a first name basis. He also caught up with a few old high school friends, which made him feel a bit awkward at times, yet for some reason he liked to know what everyone else was doing.

His biggest surprise about working at One More Cup was the random notes and gifts he'd been given. One day he found a note in the tip jar that read, *"Ethan, I love your dimples. Call me. 555-6589."* That little note made him feel good, but he never called. He had customers ask him his age and whether he was dating anyone, only to come back later to try to set him up. Ethan was attractive, not in the GQ or tall and glamorous way like Johnny, but he had his own assets. He was naturally thick and muscular, had green eyes, wavy sand colored hair, and a gentle demeanor.

There was one reason in particular that made every morning worth getting up so early to serve coffee. That reason just walked up to the counter.

Ethan smiled, feeling his stomach start to tighten. "Hey, Amy, how's your morning going?"

She was wearing a jean skirt, which had caught Ethan's eye as soon as she'd walked in. A black purse was draped over her left shoulder, wrinkling her white blouse and she carried a rolled-up newspaper in her right hand. She had light brown hair and a wide smile that cut through all of the conversations in the room.

"Hi Ethan," she said. "My morning has been fine, I guess."

Ethan had been waiting for this moment all morning. She looked beautiful. "What can I get for you?" he asked.

"I'll just have my usual."

He smiled and turned to grab the milk out of the refrigerator. "Grande vanilla latte."

"You've got it."

This morning unfolded just like the past thirty mornings. Ethan made small talk learning valuable bits and pieces about her he hoped to use soon. It was only a matter of time before he'd gather the courage to ask her out.

There was still a quite a bit he didn't know about her such as what food she liked, her favorite color or if she was dating anyone. He obviously had no clue whether she would even want to go out with him. Johnny always made fun of him for being clueless about women. For years Johnny preached at Ethan to look for signs, ask certain questions, and most of all, to watch the eyes. Ethan never did figure any of that out. In a month's time, Ethan and Amy had stuck with short conversations - all of them taking place while she waited for her coffee.

Amy was still fumbling through her purse looking for her wallet as Ethan set her drink on the counter. She quickly piled a tiny mirror, three packs of cinnamon gum, a travel pack of Kleenex and lip gloss on top of the newspaper she set on the counter.

She wrinkled her forehead. "I'm sorry, I feel like an idiot, but I can't find my money." She forced a smile. "Can you take a debit card or credit card?"

Ethan grinned. "No, I can't actually, but don't sweat it, I'll cover it."

She looked down at the counter, then into his eyes. "No, no, no. I can't have you do that. Can you put it on a tab for me until tomorrow?"

Ethan was devouring every second of this event. He couldn't get enough of the look on her face. "Seriously, don't worry about it," he said. "I'll take care of it."

She smiled and began filling her purse with the things she'd just taken out. "You're too sweet."

Ethan noticed her cheeks were flush. He felt as though he had gained some serious ground with her. As he watched her fill her purse, he glanced at the newspaper on the counter. Once he saw it he couldn't remove his eyes from the headline.

"Forty Years to the Day – One Month Away." The article began, *"The Palm Sunday Outbreak, no*

one could have predicted it."

"Ethan, are you okay?" asked Amy.

He shook his head quickly. "Huh?"

Amy's lips parted as her eyebrows scrunched together. "What's wrong? What is it?"

Ethan pointed to the article.

"Oh, I know. Isn't that weird?" She zipped her purse, then looked at Ethan. "Have you ever heard about what happened?"

Ethan leaned his elbows on the counter. "Yeah, my dad has some old newspaper clippings."

Amy draped her purse over her shoulder. "Really?"

Ethan perused the pastries beneath the glass. "Actually, his parents were killed by those tornadoes."

She dropped her hand to the glass counter. "Oh, I'm sorry."

"No, it's okay. I really don't know much about what happened, which makes me wonder why I don't."

Amy pressed a lid on top of her coffee, then grabbed it in her right hand. "My grandpa wrote a book about it," she said.

Ethan raised his eyebrows. "I'd be interested to read what he wrote sometime if you wouldn't mind."

"No, not at all." She shifted her weight. "Actually, why don't you let me buy you a cup of coffee?" She grinned. "Then I can pay you back and we can look through that book."

Ethan smiled as his insides did a somersault. "That sounds good."

"What about Thursday afternoon? Let's say about 3:30. Meet right here?"

Ethan nodded, and then took a mental picture of Amy's sea-green eyes, knowing he'd think of them often.

CHAPTER 4

David hunched over in front of his mother gasping for air. A ring of sweat surrounded his neck and arm pits.

"What's wrong?" she asked, leaping out of her chair. "David, what's wrong?" she asked again. The chair clamored to the floor.

David braced his arms on his knees. Still fighting for air, he lifted his head toward his mother. "Where's dad?"

David's lungs burned. He grabbed his ribs as though trying to wipe away a sharp pain.

His mother placed her hand on his back. "Are

you okay?" she asked.

David stood up straight, his hand still on his ribs. He looked his mother square in the eyes. "Where is he?"

She pointed upstairs. "He's taking a nap. Now, slow down and talk to me."

David scrunched his eyebrows together, his forehead wrinkled. "Haven't you looked outside?"

David's mother turned toward the kitchen window. He leaped up the stairs to his father's bedroom. He swung the door open. His father squirmed under the covers.

David fought for air, grabbing his side even harder. "Dad! Dad! Get up!"

His father sat up. He blinked repeatedly, looking around the room. Finally, his eyes found David's.

The rush of blood filling David's cheeks tingled. "Look outside!" He yanked open the curtains of the window at the foot of the bed.

David's father crawled forward and peered out the window. Charcoal clouds lined in gray had overtaken the blue and yellow of the sky. The clouds rumbled against each other, stirring slowly, boiling upward. Winds howled as they bent trees sideways toward the east. Pellets of hail plastered the window, making both David and his father flinch.

David's father jumped out of bed. A vein bulged from the middle of his forehead. "To the basement! Get your sister!"

David found Rebecca on the floor in the middle of her bedroom. She was playing with her teddy bears amongst a pile of clothes, her dolls, and a wooden rocking chair.

"Come here, Rebecca," he said. He reached his arms out toward her. "We're going down to the basement."

"David, come on!" his father yelled up the stairway.

Rebecca looked at David, then back at her teddy bears and started crying.

David placed his hands on her shoulders. He took a deep breath. "You can bring one if you want to." He pointed toward the bears. As though he had pushed a magic button, she stopped crying. "Which one do you want?"

"That one." She pointed to a well-worn fuzzy bear with a heart sewn on its chest.

David handed it to her, then scurried down the stairs. A barrage of debris plastered the house as he ran. Two windows crashed in right behind him.

As though they had practiced this before, David's father reached for the handle to the basement door just as David rounded the corner. His father carried a flashlight and radio and his mother had two blankets.

Wood snapped all around them tossing millions of tiny spears into the air. The light above them exploded as shredded metal went flying through the ceiling. Then, in one motion, the walls surrounding David twisted and lifted like the top of a cookie jar. A cloud of dust overtook all visibility as debris plastered David across the face from all directions. The scent of gas punched David in the nose, and then left as quickly as it came. Winds swirled pushing against his shoulders and his chest at the same time. David held Rebecca tight as he fought his way down the stairs.

Seconds turned into hours.

Rebecca kicked David in the stomach and screamed into his chest. He wouldn't let her head up. "It's okay, I've got you!" he said.

As he finally reached the very bottom step, he felt a jolt from under his legs. The very steps beneath him began to rise. He lost his balance and began falling toward the cement of the basement floor. He managed to turn his body so he'd land on his back cradling Rebecca.

He caught a glimpse of his parents as he fell. A vein in his mother's neck bulged below her wide-open mouth, but he couldn't hear anything other than his own breathing. His father looked frozen in place, his eyes spread wide. His mother turned toward his father and threw herself into his arms.

A swirl of brown and black climbed directly above them. Through a cloudy haze David could see a faint ray of sun angling toward one side of the funnel. That's when he saw his parents for the very last time. Without a goodbye, the stairway yanked loose and flew straight up toward heaven, then it disintegrated.

David's left shoulder felt the brunt of the cement floor first. Then, a pain shot up his lower back.

He gathered all of his strength and thrust his body upward, then opened his eyes. He sat up in bed entangled in the blankets. Trails of sweat lined the edges of his face.

"David."

Thunder echoed as flashes of light lit up the bedroom.

Finally realizing where he was, he wiped his face with both hands and exhaled as though he'd been holding his breath.

"Honey," said Jeanne.

He didn't say a word.

Jeanne touched the side of his cheek with the back of her hand, rubbing it up and down gently. "Anything I can do?" she asked.

He pulled the covers to the side, walked to the window, and glanced out at the storm. "No, I'm fine," he said, then staggered out of the bedroom.

CHAPTER 5

A stream of lights flew by on Main Street right in front of Ethan. It was Tuesday night and he was in the parking lot at the old Armory. As he waited, he read all the illuminated business signs. The pubs, jewelry stores, and flower shops still looked the same. He wondered how they'd managed to stick around all these years.

The Armory has been abandoned for over thirty years. The broken windows, old wooden floors and crumbling brick gave Ethan and Johnny exactly what they wanted. This good for nothing building became their stomping grounds. Originally, they met on the roof, which meant climbing the steel fire escape, busting open a hatch, shimmying up on top of it, and then pulling themselves over the edge. However, after Ethan nearly fell through the sagging roof, they decided to try a new spot along the bank of the river. They soon discovered how much they liked fishing.

A Nissan Pathfinder pulled into the parking lot, spotless with shiny wheels carrying a driver with a huge white smile. Johnny had drooled over that Pathfinder for months. It was the summary of what he stood for; he always got what he wanted. His perfectly mapped-out plan had worked. He lived it up at college, found his wife, moved back home to work in the recreational vehicle industry, and then started a family. Middlebury, and the surrounding towns, is considered the RV capital of the world. Johnny is a sales rep for the top company, of which his father happens to be the vice president. Johnny is a schmoozer.

Sometimes Johnny makes Ethan sick. They come from such opposite ends of the spectrum. Ethan's family knows what it means to reheat the pot roast they'd eaten the night before. Oddly enough, his father was once the vice president of sales at an RV company, but that ended fifteen years ago when jobs were hard to find and harder to keep. His father spent two years technically unemployed, but worked at a farm to make ends meet. Since then, he'd had numerous jobs while trying to find a company where he could slide into the very position he'd worked at before. But no matter how hard he worked, proving himself all over again, he hadn't been given another opportunity. Ethan knew what it was like to have money be the center of a household argument. Johnny wouldn't know what that was like. Ethan didn't resent Johnny because he came from a wealthy family, but sometimes he wished his friend knew what his life was like.

Johnny hopped out of his new truck carrying a brown paper bag. Ethan's S10 felt small as he got out.

They gave each other a quick one-armed hug and began walking toward the backside of the Armory.

"What's in there?" asked Ethan. He nodded toward the bag.

Johnny smiled, proud of himself. "What do you think it is?"

Ethan laughed. "You didn't."

Johnny shook his head. "I sure did."

During their college summer breaks they began drinking a Hornsby from time to time out at the Armory. Hornsby, apple cider with a kick, is Ethan's favorite drink, mainly because he can't stand the taste of beer. They didn't drink much, just on occasions when they were going to talk about old times. Tonight, apparently, was going to be one of those nights.

"Do you remember the Johnson Street Bridge?"

asked Johnny.

Ethan grinned as he relived a movie reel of memories in an instant. "Sure do. How could I not?"

"We must have been bored out of our minds."

Ethan and Johnny sat on the grass at the top of the bank of the river, just as they had all the times before.

"I can't believe we just waited there on top of the bridge under that burned out light until a cop saw us," said Johnny.

"Yeah, and then we'd take off running for no reason at all."

They laughed in unison.

Johnny pulled a Hornsby out of the bag, twisted the top off and handed it to Ethan. Then he opened one for himself.

"I can still hear the engine of the squad car rev as they'd come chasing after us," said Johnny. He grinned at Ethan. "And the light, that dang spotlight of a flashlight."

Ethan shook his head. "Do you remember that time we were racing through Mr. Anderson's corn field? And you got clothes-lined by that barbed wire fence?"

Johnny nodded. "Oh yeah, I remember that. I couldn't see a thing. I had no idea it was there."

Ethan took a swig and let out a deep breath. "You got so lucky."

Johnny wrinkled his forehead. "What are you

talking about?"

Ethan tilted his head. "How did you come out of that without a scratch on you, even landing on your feet?" asked Ethan.

"That took some talent, I admit it." Johnny had a smirk of accomplishment on his face. "Do you remember where we ended up running to? How we hid from the cops that time?"

He looked at the label on his drink, then at Johnny. "I can't remember."

Johnny raised his bottle. "Think eighth grade, your first love."

Ethan laughed. "Melinda Lane." He clinked his bottle against Johnny's.

"Yep, the girl that stole both of our first kisses."

Ethan shook his head and smiled. "But I guess you won that one, because you kissed her first."

They watched the river move as it shifted the lights it was reflecting.

Johnny took a drink, then exhaled. "Speaking of Melinda Lane, I'm glad that didn't work out for you."

Ethan looked at him, amused. "Yeah, things looked like they were going to be for the long haul up until ninth grade." He smirked. "Should I even ask?"

"Ask what?"

"Where that came from?"

"Well it just so happens that we have a new administrative assistant in the office. She's drop dead gorgeous and as sweet as can be," Johnny said. "Think Melinda Lane, but fifteen years older."

Ethan shrugged his shoulders. "What is it with you?" he asked. "Why are you always trying to set me up with someone?"

"How else are you going to get a date?"

Ethan took a swig. "Yeah, that's funny."

"Well," Johnny hesitated, "do you have any other options that I don't know about?"

"I might."

Johnny turned directly toward Ethan. "All right buddy, who is she?"

Ethan cleared his throat. "Her name is Amy."

"That's it? Does she have a last name?"

Ethan exhaled. "I think it's Yoder."

"You think?"

"Listen, she's a girl that comes into the coffee shop almost every day and tomorrow is the first time we're going to sit down and talk."

Impressed, Johnny nodded. "Nice work." Then he looked up into the sky. "Amy Yoder, I've heard that name before."

"You have?"

Ethan was somewhat surprised. But then again, Johnny had always been the sort of person that could remember the name of nearly anyone he'd met since he was in sixth grade.

"She was second runner-up for the county fair queen three years after we graduated from high school," he said, and then grinned. "Well, that is if it's the same Amy Yoder."

Ethan counted the difference in age in his head. "So that would mean she was a senior in high school the same year we were seniors in college?"

"Yep, which probably means she just graduated from college last year." Johnny smiled, pleased with himself. "You've got yourself a young one."

Ethan looked down at the river, then took another drink.

For the next hour the two of them sat on the edge of the riverbank talking about women, old jobs, and some of the pranks they pulled off in college. They laughed for an hour about everything, reliving the stories as though they had happened yesterday.

As they were getting ready to leave, Johnny opened the passenger door to his Pathfinder and grabbed a white plastic bag.

Ethan was digging out his keys when Johnny held out the plastic bag.

"What's this?" asked Ethan.

"Just take it. There might be something useful in here." Johnny laughed under his breath.

Ethan grabbed the bag, opened it and pulled out a *Men's Health Magazine*. The top headline read, *No Longer Clueless*. Ethan shook his head in disbelief. He tossed the magazine in his truck.

"You're such a punk."

Johnny patted Ethan on the shoulder. "I saw it today and it reminded me of you." He smiled. "I'm just trying to help my boy out."

"Whatever."

Johnny leaned in and gave Ethan a one-armed hug.

Ethan hopped in his truck. "The Armory was a good idea."

"Well, we're going to have to do this more often." Johnny nodded toward him. "It's good to have you back."

CHAPTER 6

Ethan sipped his cherry Sprite as he waited for
Amy. He tried to read the newspaper, but his eyes
kept glancing toward the door. A bell jingled above
it every time it opened. He'd sat at a table for two,
snug against the wall, facing the door.

The few people in One More Cup all knew him.
He'd said his hellos, then managed to keep to
himself. He tried all of the sections of the paper, but
nothing held his attention. He wondered if anyone
in there was watching him. They probably would
have noticed him wiping his palms on his pants.
This was his only chance to leave a first impression.

Even though they had spoken almost every morning for the past month, this was it.

Why was he so nervous?

Ethan had experienced his share of first dates, but he'd never gotten this nervous. He tried on three different outfits before picking a red button-down shirt and his favorite jeans. There wasn't any reason to be nervous; this wasn't even technically a date. They were just going to talk about what happened on April 11, 1965, and that might be it. That was, after all, what he really wanted to talk about. But then again, he'd found himself attracted to Amy ever since her first vanilla latte.

He took another glance at the door, then opened the sports section. *What if he did actually like Amy? What if she was exactly what he'd been looking for all these years?* Ethan found himself smiling every time he thought about her. *That meant something, right?* She was always sweet to him, and he couldn't get enough of her eyes.

Was he really ready to invest the time and effort it took to build a relationship? There's always the chance it won't work out, then look at all that lost time. He wasn't looking to date around and have a good time with someone. He was getting older, hopefully wiser, and was ready to find that someone to wake up to each morning. Amy was, most likely, only twenty-two. She might not be ready for that kind of commitment yet.

"Hey, Ethan."

That was the soft, sweet voice he'd been waiting for.

Ethan had lost himself staring at an article about steroid use in baseball. He wanted to see her first, not be seen. He quickly folded the newspaper in half, set it on top of the table, and stood up.

He offered his hand. "Hi Amy," he said. He tried his best to smile comfortably.

She shook his hand with the lightest of touch. Ethan's stomach churned, realizing that was the first time they'd touched. They smiled and sat down at the same time. She'd worn a three-quarter-sleeved white T-shirt, denim capris, and white sliders. Once again, she'd taken his breath away.

"Wow, you shaved." She smiled broadly.

Most mornings Ethan was covered in scruff and his eyes were hidden by a Chicago Cubs baseball cap. He wondered if she'd notice.

"Yeah, and I didn't even cut myself." He grinned. "Anyway, how was the classroom today?" he asked.

She set a brown purse on the floor beside the table. "We had a big test today, which the kids hated me for, but from what I could see they all did pretty well." She smiled and breathed a sigh of relief. "What about you? How was the rest of your morning? You seemed really busy when I saw you."

He folded the newspaper into quarters in front of him.

"It was crazy for a while, but that made the time

fly by, so I didn't mind." Ethan's shoestrings made
a faint repetitive tapping noise as he bounced his leg
up and down. A habit that shows up during tests,
intense games, and any other time he got anxious.
He didn't notice the sound until he saw Amy
grinning. Then, his face grew red and the noise
stopped.

Ethan turned to see two customers waiting at the
counter. He looked back at Amy. "Can I buy you a
drink or a muffin or something?"

Amy noticed he'd shaved since the morning.
Some mornings when she saw him, his face was
covered in whiskers and his eyes were hidden
underneath a Cubs baseball cap. But this afternoon,
as she looked at him, she saw the deep green of his
eyes, which made her feel as though she knew him
better than she did. "Actually, I'm fine. But thanks
for offering."

"Are you sure you don't want anything?"

Amy shook her head from side to side. "No
thanks. I just had a Diet Coke."

Ethan smirked.

"What?"

"You and my mom both."

Amy wrinkled her forehead.

"She loves Diet Coke, drinks it everyday. I
don't know how you guys do it, because there isn't
any taste to it."

Amy grinned. "There aren't any calories
either."

"That's what my mom says too."

"And let me guess, she goes to Curves." Curves, a circuit training for women, focuses on a quick, cardio, total-body workout.

Ethan smiled, letting out a slight laugh. "Of course she does. She's got to be on top of what's popular around here."

Amy nodded in agreement. "I just started going this week. Well, my mom and I are going together. It's so much fun, and it is a good workout."

"You know what's funny? Curves has been out in Denver for at least four years, and it's just now getting started here. I guess that's what happens when you live in small-town, Indiana."

Amy's mouth widened as much as her eyes did in surprise. "So you lived in Denver?"

"I sure did. I moved out there right after college."

"Where'd you go?"

"Purdue."

"I went to Indiana."

"Looks like we're bitter enemies," Ethan teased.

"It sure does."

As their conversation continued, Ethan realized he had finally relaxed. He joked about her addiction to vanilla lattes - she hadn't missed a single morning for over a month. He also talked about himself when he was asked. He told her that he was an engineer, about his job in Denver, and how it's been nice to get used to life in his hometown again.

Amy seemed comfortable too. Her elbows were on the tabletop, as she rested her hands underneath her chin. She did get a little red in the face when he asked her about being second runner-up at the county fair. She was adorable, twirling her hair, as she spoke about the song she sang for her talent, *This Kiss*, by Faith Hill. She rolled her eyes as she described how her mother had all but forced her to enter the competition because there was scholarship money at stake. Ethan's guess about her age was confirmed when she told him the year of the competition. She had graduated exactly four years after him, making her twenty-two, and in her first year of teaching.

She was young, but what did age really matter? That's what he kept asking himself.

The bell above the door to the coffee shop had been jingling off and on ever since Ethan and Amy sat down. Neither of them had paid much attention to the traffic. They were wrapped up in their conversation, getting to know each other. An hour passed and neither had brought up anything about the tornado or the book her grandfather had written. Ethan was about to bring it up when he happened to see Johnny walk in.

He was beaming. As he walked closer, he lifted his eyebrows up and down, making faces, trying to get Ethan to laugh. All Ethan could think was *Please don't come over here. Don't come over here. Oh crap.*

The next thing Ethan knew, Johnny was standing beside their table.

"Hey Johnny," Ethan said as he stood up to greet him. He leaned in close giving him a one-armed hug. Then he whispered, "Say hi, and leave, or I will beat you."

Johnny smiled, as Ethan stepped away.

"Johnny, this is Amy. Amy, Johnny."

"Nice to meet you," they both said as they shook hands.

"Johnny is my best friend."

"Oh, I see," she said.

"Anytime you really want to know something about Ethan, you just let me know. I think I've got a story or two for you." Johnny seemed proud of himself for making Amy smile and Ethan feel helpless. "I could tell you about Ethan running a naked lap around the dorm or about the time some buddies strung his whitey-tighties together and hung them out the window."

Ethan shook his head from side to side, trying to manage a grin.

"I'll have to keep that in mind," she said. Amy was grinning, she obviously enjoyed watching Ethan squirm.

Then Johnny said good-bye to both of them and walked over to the line of people waiting to order a drink.

"Don't ask." Ethan muttered.

"I'll bet you two are quite the tandem together."

"I guess you could say that." Ethan agreed. "We've had some good times."

"I wish my best friend lived around here. That would be nice."

"Where does she live? If I may presume it's a she?"

"She," Amy smiled, "lives in South Carolina."

"At least you have a great excuse to go out there."

"That's true. Actually, my friends and I had a New Year's Eve party out there, right on the ocean, in Charleston." She flipped through a photo album of memories frozen in her mind. "It was beautiful."

A few moments later, Johnny waved to both of them as he walked toward the door. He turned around, at a point where only Ethan could see him, and gave him a thumbs-up along with a wink. When the door shut behind him, Ethan remembered what he was going to ask Amy before Johnny ever walked in.

He cleared his throat. "Did you bring the book?"

Amy squirmed in her seat as though she was guilty of something. "I was waiting for you to ask that." She tilted her head slightly as though hoping to be forgiven. "I forgot it. I'm sorry."

Ethan tried to look at her condescendingly, but he quickly wiped that away with a smile. "I guess I can let it slide this time."

"I really am sorry. I want to show you the book

and see what you think of it."

"I'd love to see it."

"I'm curious. So what do you know about the tornadoes? Can I ask?"

Ethan shifted in his seat, his face suddenly serious. "Uh, not a whole lot. My dad has never been able to talk about it. And my mother doesn't want to try to tell me what he experienced. So, I only know what I've read in a few newspaper articles."

Amy's eyes widened. "Really?"

"I've tried to talk to my dad, but I think he blames himself somehow, and I can't figure out why."

"Has he said that? That he blames himself?"

"No, he hasn't, but he's had nightmares about it for as long as I can remember." Ethan flipped the newspaper over on its other side as though looking for something to do. "I just want to talk to him about it. I want to know what happened to my grandparents, but most of all to him. Maybe it will help. I know it would be great for me. Then maybe I'll be able to understand some things about why he's the way he is. You know what I mean?"

Amy's eyes looked soft and comforting. "I do know what you mean."

When the conversation seemed to be winding down, Ethan's palms became damp again, his neck felt itchy and his stomach tightened. He had to ask Amy out on a date. He gathered every nerve in his body that he could find, and went for it.

"Would you have dinner with me tomorrow night?"

Amy seemed pleasantly surprised.

CHAPTER 7

Later that evening Ethan was upstairs, sifting through boxes in what was supposed to be the guest bedroom, but instead had turned into the biggest storage room in the house. He'd been browsing through what he thought were the oldest boxes in the room, hoping he'd find one that had anything from his father's childhood. No luck so far. What he'd found were boxes upon boxes of clothes, filed paperwork, and his old toys: Transformers, M.A.S.K., G.I. Joe men, and Matchbox cars. He'd also found trophies from his little league baseball days along with ribbons from the 4-H fair.

He heard a car door shut so he quickly folded the box he was looking through and peeked out the blinds. He breathed softly, seeing his mother, and went downstairs to meet her.

"Hey mom."

She gave him her normal tight hug, then set her bag on the kitchen table. She saw an envelope with her name on it and picked it up.

"How were the kids today?" asked Ethan.

Jeanne taught sixth grade English at the middle school. She'd been there for twenty-five years, teaching the same subject every year.

"Oh, they were fine. You know how kids are. They start to get antsy when the sun is shining and it looks warm outside."

"It sure was nice out today, wasn't it?"

"Yes it was."

Ethan sat down at the kitchen table. He watched as Jeanne read the note his father had written her. She smiled, folded the note and put it back in the envelope. Ethan didn't ask about the note. He knew better than to pry, and besides, he didn't want to know.

Jeanne continued to smile as she opened the refrigerator and grabbed a Diet Coke.

Ethan cleared his throat. "Did you see the paper today?"

Jeanne ran her hand through her hair. "No, why?"

"I just wondered because there's an article about

the tornado again."

"Really?" Jeanne sat down at the kitchen table across from Ethan, opened her soda and waited for him to continue.

"I saw it this morning at the coffee shop. I picked up another copy on my way home. Do you want to read it?" asked Ethan.

"Sure," she said.

Ethan went to his bedroom, grabbed the paper off his bed, then took it to his mother. She turned straight to the article and began reading.

Ethan went back upstairs to the storage room. Finally, he spotted a shoebox wedged in between two larger ones. "Newspaper clippings," was written on the side in his father's handwriting."

Once before when Ethan was fourteen he'd found that same box. But before he could read any of the articles, his father found him and made it very clear that box was off limits. That was the first time Ethan had seen the vein in his father's forehead bulge and his nerves rattled

He maneuvered the shoebox free and set it on top of a stack of other boxes chest-high in front of him. Ethan pulled off the top and peaked in. He uncovered hundreds of yellow newspaper clippings with faded, barely readable typeset. He picked them up one by one. Each clipping felt like a dried leaf, crusty, and frail. Headlines read, *"Full Storm Story," "A Night of Horror," "At Least 75 Killed."* Ethan flipped through the clippings catching words and reading paragraphs from random sections of each story. He uncovered another headline that read, *"Many Missing After Tornado."* The very next one underneath that one made him freeze where he was, *"The Death List."* There were two hundred and fifty six names listed.

"Did you find what you were looking for?"

Ethan's heart sank and blood raced through his body. He turned his head toward the doorway. He spotted his father was leaning against the frame, watching him.

David stood just over six feet tall, lean, with a small belly dangling over his belt. His Adam's apple protruded sharply and he almost always had a five o clock shadow across his weathered face. His hands were worn, nicked up and scarred from years of hard, physical labor.

"Almost, but it looks like the police caught me." Ethan glanced at the clippings in his hand, then his father.

David walked toward him, eyeing the shoebox. "Let me guess, you saw the article in the newspaper today?"

"Yeah, I did." Ethan handed the clippings to his father. "Since you've never let me near this shoebox, I figured it was time I found out for myself what happened."

Instead of responding, David simply began placing the newspaper clippings back into the shoebox in an orderly stack. When the articles were in their correct spot, he placed the lid on top of the shoebox.

"I'll tell you when the time is right," said David.

"I'm twenty-six-years old, Dad. I think I can handle it."

"You're not the one I'm concerned about."

"You know, sometimes I feel like I barely know you." Ethan clenched his jaw. "I just don't get why it's so hard to talk about. I don't know why you have those dreams. I don't even know what they are. I can't believe you can't talk to me about this."

David placed the box in the corner, underneath a stack of other boxes where Ethan found it.

"I have talked about this before and nothing good came out of it."

"You just don't get it, do you?" Ethan raised his arms. "There's always been this mysterious, distant side of you. I feel like I've been cheated, robbed of my dad. As far as I can tell, there's no one to blame but you."

David didn't look up or respond. He turned and walked away.

CHAPTER 8

That same night Ethan and his mother lounged around in the living room. Jeanne sat on the recliner, reading the latest novel of her favorite author. Ethan wrapped himself in an afghan and sprawled out on the couch to watch TV. The show tested people against their fears and inhibitions. Ethan soaked in every minute of it. He wished he could be a contestant.

"Your father told me he saw you looking through his box upstairs."

Ethan looked at her as if to say, "So what."

"That's all he's got, you know."

Ethan rolled his head toward his mother and exhaled. "What?"

"That's all he's got from the tornado." She paused, glancing at Ethan. "Everything he ever owned, ever had, was blown away."

Ethan watched the television not really paying attention to what was on anymore. His insides burned to get all of this out in the open.

"Why has dad never been able to talk about it? I hardly know anything that happened that day." He paused, racing through his memories.

Jeanne set her book in her lap. "It was a terrible day. Lots of people around here still remember it. You know," she hesitated, "he tried to tell you what happened."

"He did?"

Jeanne nodded. "Yep, when you were sixteen. Do you remember when he took you fishing?"

"Of course I do, that was the only time he ever took me fishing. We stayed in a log cabin on a lake somewhere up in Canada."

Ethan recalled the twelve-hour trip, straight north, until they reached a dirt trail that lead to the cabin. He counted seven black bears, spotted a moose, and even spied a bald eagle. They fished twice a day, took naps in between, and ate what they caught. Ethan loved to chop wood for the wood stove that heated the entire cabin. Everything was wood - the flooring, the walls, the ceiling, the dinner table, and even the furniture. It was a "man's getaway," and happened to belong to David's boss, who insisted he take Ethan.

It was their first weeklong trip, only the two of them. David joked they needed to be out on the lake before the fish woke up. So, each morning, Ethan layered sweatshirts and jackets to endure the brisk boat ride. Once they were at the perfect spot, they tossed their fishing lines in and waited.

There was one particular moment Ethan never forgot. He and his father were fishing before dusk. David was leaning back on his chair near the motor with his hands clasped together behind his head. He steadily eyed his fishing pole propped up against the side of the boat. Ethan's feet rested on the front ledge of the boat. He was holding his fishing pole, waiting for the slightest nibble. The water reflected the orange and purple of the setting sun. The only sound around was the chatter of birds. Ethan wiped his nose, catching a whiff of the lake water, when David began to talk.

David told Ethan about the estate planning he and Jeanne had just finished; it was all gibberish to Ethan. Then he went on to mention a will. Ethan sat in disbelief as his father instructed him what to do in case he died. There weren't any health concerns to worry about, no diseases to be fought; he just wanted Ethan to be prepared.

"Your father was going to tell you on that trip."

"Why didn't he?" asked Ethan.

Jeanne pulled the recliner up. "He said every

time he brought it up, it just never felt right to talk about." She pulled off her reading glasses and wiped her nose. "I think he didn't want to depress you, and most of all, he didn't want you to feel sorry for him."

Ethan turned his head toward her. "Why would I feel sorry for him?"

She looked into Ethan's eyes. "Because of what happened."

Ethan sighed. "Well can you tell me what happened?"

Jeanne didn't answer. Ethan turned his attention toward the television. He sat in silence, frustrated.

Jeanne put her glasses back on, read one page, then took them off again. "Did you know the President was here?"

Ethan smirked. "Here? In Middlebury?"

"Yep, President Lyndon B. Johnson."

"Wow." Ethan's scrunched his eyebrows together. "But, why was he here?"

"Because the tornadoes that came through caused so much damage and killed so many people, that it was one of the largest tornado tragedies in the history of the United States." She looked up at the ceiling, reeling through her memories of that day.

Ethan sat up and placed the afghan across his lap. "Where were you when all of that happened?"

Jeanne crossed her legs. "On my way to church."

"Did you see a tornado?"

"Yep." Jeanne closed the book she was holding.
"I'll never forget it." She began rocking back and
forth. She stared at the book cover, finding her way
back to that day so long ago. "It was such a muggy,
humid, miserable day. Mom and I were on our way
to an evening church service. A quartet was
supposed to sing, so Dad didn't want to go. He
stayed home. I can still see him standing on the
steps, waving as we left."

Jeanne exhaled. "As mom was driving, I
remember looking out the window and watching a
perfect blue sky be overtaken by enormous, grayish-
green clouds." She traced her fingers over the cover
of the book. She looked up, finding Ethan's eyes on
her. "We were just about to church when we noticed
a bunch of people pulled to the side of the road.
They were out of their cars watching the sky as if
waiting for a spaceship to appear. There was a man
standing outside his car snapping pictures of the
whole thing."

Ethan's lips parted, envisioning that moment.

"Mom pulled over just down the road from him.
We both got out too. I stood beside her because
something didn't feel right to me. I think she felt it
too."

Jeanne ran her hand along the binding of the
book. "It was amazing to watch those clouds. They
kept growing higher and darker, yet everything
around us was still. I didn't feel any wind, not even
a breeze." She paused, taking a breath. "Then, out

of nowhere, a loud rumble crashed above us and huge balls of ice fell from the sky. We covered our heads like this," she ducked and interlocked her hands over her head. "We leaped back into the car. Luckily, we didn't get hit."

She exhaled. "I can still hear the force of those things pounding our car."

Jeanne flipped over the book she was holding, touching it as though analyzing the texture.

Ethan leaned in, placing his elbows on his knees and his hands on his chin.

"When the hail stopped, I opened my door and picked up one of those ice balls. It was literally the size of a softball." She made the outline of a softball with her hands. "Mom and I couldn't believe the size of it." She raised her eyebrows toward Ethan. "One of those ice balls cracked my side of the windshield. We were so lucky it didn't brake. The roof and hood were covered in dents."

Jeanne took a deep breath. "For some reason, I remember watching mom glance out the window as she started the car. Her face went pale. I was still holding that ice ball when mom calmly started the car and pulled us onto the highway, heading away from church. When I asked where we were going, she calmly said that we were going home." Jeanne's eyes watered up.

"Within minutes, I watched a tornado dangle from the sky, as though it was dancing, then it touched the ground almost exactly where we were parked. Then, out of nowhere, there were four other tornadoes on the ground behind that one. It seemed like they were working together to chase us down." Jeanne's eyes widened. "I still can't believe what I saw next." She sniffed. "All of those tornadoes came together to form one. That tornado must have been a half-mile wide." She looked at Ethan intently. "I saw it completely demolish our church, suck up an entire lake, and flatten a row of trailer homes. Power converters exploded into huge fireballs. I felt like I was in a war zone."

She inhaled, calming herself. "I watched a family die."

Ethan wrinkled his forehead and shook his head.

"The father was holding a child in one arm and pulling open a cellar door with the other. His wife was right behind him. I screamed because I could see the tornado coming right at them. Then, their entire house blew up. In an instant, everything was gone, including the family." Jeanne wiped her brow, as though trying to chase that image away.

She continued, "I also vividly remember watching a cow fall from the sky, a silo, and half of a pick up truck too. That tornado must have followed us for ten miles before it vanished into the sky, like it was never there."

She inhaled. "Mom and I wanted to go help whoever we could, but we saw another tornado about three miles away coming in our direction." Jeanne pressed her lips together. "We left without helping all of those people. They needed us."

Ethan remained silent, unsure of what to say.

After a brief lull, Jeanne continued, "When we got home dad already had the cellar doors open and was watching for us. He said he had a feeling church would be cancelled." She smirked, shaking her head. "We had just closed one of the cellar doors when we saw a tornado, about 100 yards wide, right across the street." She paused, catching her breath. "Our cellar was cold, musty, and completely dark. I always hated to go down there."

She glanced down at the shiny hardwood flooring, then back at Ethan. "Do you really want to know what happened?"

Ethan's lips parted. "Are you kidding me? Of course I do."

Jeanne folded her hands, set them on top of her book, and began rubbing her thumbs together. "I had to listen to a tornado demolish our neighbors' houses. It sounded like a freight train was driving right over them. I clung to Mom, who was covered by Dad. All I could hear was wind howling as though a blow dryer was blasting right into my ear. That sound came and went so fast and was replaced with screams." Jeanne looked up at the ceiling. "After dad checked to make sure the coast was clear, we climbed out. I couldn't believe my eyes." She shook her head. "The entire row of houses across the street, all fourteen of them, were gone. They were just huge piles of rubble. There were dead bodies scattered, cars turned over, houses on fire, and trees broken in half, their tops nowhere to be found. I saw a man in our lawn wrapped in telephone wire, like he'd been caught in a huge spider web. And I'll never forget the pieces of straw sticking in the lone telephone pole still standing, as though someone had thrown a set of darts."

Ethan shook his head.

"Dad made mom and me stay near the cellar for fear of another tornado. I watched as he ran to each demolished house, yelling, calling out names. Three other men quickly joined him. Together, they pulled out ten people."

Ethan paused, soaking it all in. "That's unbelievable, Mom."

Jeanne continued rubbing her thumbs together. "That was such a long night." She sighed. "We opened up our house to our neighbors. I spent most of my time bandaging people. But honestly, the worst part of that whole night for me was that I had no idea where your father was. I had no way of getting a hold of him and my parents weren't about to let me go over to his house by myself. I was a wreck, crying constantly. Finally, at about midnight, my dad took me in his truck over to David's house." Jeanne lowered her head. "That drive was awful. It was pitch black. There were power lines down everywhere. A number of houses were simply gone. My father actually drove past David's house because we couldn't tell where it was, or where it was supposed to be."

Jeanne stared at her hands.

"There was nothing there. No cars, no animals, no barn, and no house. I yelled and yelled for him, shining the flashlight. Dad was frantically searching through debris, hoping for the best. We were out there for over an hour." She looked up at Ethan. "Finally, dad grabbed me and held me. I cried so hard. He told me we'd go the hospital first thing in the morning."

Jeanne wiped her eyes. "That was the emptiest feeling I've ever had. I thought your father was dead."

Ethan closed his eyes. "Mom, I'm sorry."

Jeanne blinked slowly, reliving the moment.

Ethan watched her eyes glaze over, staring into space.

She shook her head, as though chasing away a thought she didn't want to think anymore. Jeanne found Ethan's eyes again. "I will never forget the following morning." She paused. "There were clouds of dirt hovering in the air."

Ethan wrinkled his forehead. "Clouds of dirt?"

She nodded. "Those tornadoes ripped up so many fields and destroyed so many things that there was so much debris in the sky, it looked like clouds." She scratched her head.

Ethan stared at the wall trying to envision that day. "So how many tornadoes were there?"

"If I remember right, there were fifty-one."

Ethan's head snapped toward her. "Fifty-one?"

A tear filled the very corner of her eye. "Yes," she sighed, "but one would have been enough for your father."

CHAPTER 9

David floated in mid-air, lying down, frozen in place. He couldn't see anything, complete darkness surrounded him.

He noticed a breeze passing by his ears, whistling softly. He looked to his right and saw nothing. He looked to his left and found nothing there either. Gradually the air gained speed   until finally he felt the force against his entire body.

Suddenly, it all stopped.

He dangled in mid-air as though on a roller coaster pausing for a split second at the peak of its highest point. Then, he felt a push in the middle of his back that made his entire body arch. Winds raced through every crevice they could find. David was simply a puppet, going wherever the winds carried him.

The deep black walls around him began to swirl with burnt charcoal. Glimpses of silver mixed in. The colors smeared together like an abstract painting.

David's veins filled with a rush of adrenaline. He saw the bottom of the stairs he'd fallen off. They twirled above and around him along with a kitchen table he'd eaten at only hours ago. He saw a dresser with no drawers, a bed with no sheets, and a sofa with no cushions, all spinning above him. That's when he realized his arms were clutching something.

It was Rebecca.

He met her tear-filled blue eyes just as his back felt the wallop of an oversized paddle. He'd landed on the cement of the basement floor. His face grimaced in agony. He would have screamed in hopes of releasing the rush of pain, but it was getting harder and harder to breathe. His chest felt heavy, as though a vice was slowly adding more pressure to it. He could feel his lungs filling with liquid. He knew he'd broken something.

The winds still swirled, blowing harder than before. Somehow he had to protect Rebecca, she was all that mattered now. If he could just cover her, then she would be sealed from the winds, the flying debris, and anything that could harm her.

Gathering every ounce of strength he had left, David thrust his body, rolling on top of Rebecca.

Thump.

A surge of pain shot up David's right arm. He ignored it. "I've got you! It's okay!" he said.

The pain of his back had now faded, relative to the surge in his arm. But none of the pain mattered, he was going to protect Rebecca.

"I've got you!" he said again.

When he found her eyes again, he saw a familiar brown he'd somehow memorized. He blinked, and looked closer. That's when he realized he was laying on top of his wife, Jeanne, not Rebecca. They were on the floor, tangled in their blankets.

As Jeanne had done so many times before, she waited until he freed himself of his dream. Then, she put her right hand on his cheek. "You've got me alright. I'm right here."

David's eyes began to fill with water. Only a single tear escaped, traveling down the side of his cheek, reaching the tip of his chin before finally letting go. Instead of acting as though nothing had happened, David lowered his head, and placed it in the crevice of her neck. Jeanne wrapped her arms around him and began tracing outlines across his back with her fingertips.

Lightening flashed and thunder rolled as they stayed entangled together on the bedroom floor.

CHAPTER 10

"You know I still have a job waiting for at the plant anytime you're ready for it." David folded the newspaper in half and tossed it on the floor beside the couch.

Since Ethan had been home, they'd already had this conversation five times. His father was a plant manager at Midwest Motors, a recreational vehicle manufacturing company. He supervised thirty-two employees, all in an assembly line. Some built wooden trusses and framing, others put together furniture. All had their specific responsibility, which was used to make the RV. Ethan worked at

the plant during high school and college summer
breaks. He knew most of the people there. He
would have made more money, but he didn't enjoy
that type of work near as much as he did the coffee
shop. He'd also feel more pressure. There'd be a
specific count of pieces he'd need to produce
everyday. It was tough, physical work, and right
now that's not was he wanted. His father wasn't too
happy with him, to say the least.

Ethan reclined in his favorite chair and turned on
the television. He shook his head. "I'll keep that in
mind."

"I could really use you." He looked at Ethan.
"You know how busy this time of year gets."

David worked hard to get to the position he was
in. He enjoyed coming home dirty, sweaty, and
feeling as though he'd taken his body to the max.
There was a sense of accomplishment that he got
from seeing the completed product. He was close to
most of the work crew and celebrated with them
when they met their quotas.

Ethan flipped through channels looking for
anything remotely interesting. "Yeah, I know dad.
I'm just going to stick with what I've got for right
now though."

David nodded his head. He knew that was the
answer he was going to hear. "Just know that it's a
standing offer."

Ethan gritted his teeth and took in a long breath
through his nose. "Thanks."

David picked up the newspaper, walked to the kitchen table, and tossed it beside a pile of unopened mail.

Ethan could tell his father was disappointed. He felt bad for the lack of conversation he'd just exerted. "So where are you and mom going tonight?"

Friday nights were date nights for Jeanne and David. Almost every weekend since they'd been married, they made sure to go out to eat somewhere. They'd been to every restaurant around, but The Eagle's Nest was their favorite place. It featured a seafood menu and with decent prices. It was also the restaurant of their first date. David and Jeanne were both romantic like that; good at remembering dates, places they'd been, and mixing in a surprise every now and then.

David leafed through the pile of mail. "I'm not sure yet, your mother hasn't been home from school."

Ethan stood up from the recliner. "Well, wherever you go, have a good time."

Ethan assumed the conversation was over. He started up the stairs to get ready for his big date. He hadn't mentioned it to either of his parents yet. He figured there wasn't anything that they needed to know.

"What are you up to tonight? Do you want to come with us?"

Ethan froze on the third step of the stairs and

turned around to see his father's eyes on him. He looked down at his feet, then up the stairs. "I'm going out to eat with a friend."

That was all he needed to say. Whenever Ethan said "friend" it meant that he was about to go on a date.

David grinned. "Oh yeah, do you know where yet?"

Ethan cleared his throat. "No, I haven't decided."

"Did you know there's a new place that opened on Grape Road in Mishawaka? I think it's called The Marketplace." Mishawaka has modern restaurants, chain stores, and a variety of things to do much like a bigger city.

The Marketplace was supposed to have every type of food imaginable. Since Ethan had no idea what type of food Amy might like this place was a sure bet. Besides, the restaurant opened only three weeks ago and everyone was talking about it.

"You know what, I think that's where we'll end up going," said Ethan.

David smiled, proud of himself.

An hour later, Ethan noticed his slick palms as he opened his truck door. He'd been thinking about the way Amy smiled at him ever since she said she'd love to go out to dinner tonight.

He took a deep breath to try and calm himself. He knocked on the door of apartment 3C. It had been a while, months, since he'd asked a girl out.

He'd always been on the shy side of the personality scope. Having to do something that took as much courage as it takes to ask someone out, made him leap out of his comfort zone, which was why he was pleasantly surprised with himself. Here he stood in front of 3C about to have a date with a beautiful young woman.

Amy opened the door. "Hey, Ethan," she said.

She looked beautiful. Amy was nearly the same height as Ethan, had the slender build of a runner, and a blend of blonde and brown hair. Her black dress shoes were spotless, which oddly caught Ethan's attention. The fade of her blue jeans wrapped around each thigh.

Ethan breathed easy. "Hi. You look great," he said.

Amy smiled. "Thanks. You look good too."

Amy had a genuine quality about her that anyone who was around her noticed. She listened intently, made comfortable eye contact, and carried herself in a way that showed she always looked out for others. All reasons why Ethan felt himself finally rid of the nerves he'd come with.

The drive to the restaurant was smooth with constant conversation. Ethan wanted to build on that as they walked through the entry of The Marketplace. A silver bar marked the boundary of the inner part of the restaurant where each customer walked through a turn counter. Once inside, Amy and Ethan were greeted by a horde of people all in line at separate islands for each style of food; Italian, Greek, Mexican, Garden-fresh, every type of food imaginable.

Amy had gotten excited when Ethan told her where they were going. She said she'd wanted to eat there ever since she heard it advertised on the radio. The Marketplace looked the size of a small cafeteria, but with higher ceilings and windows on all sides. There stood trees, flowers, uneven bricks as the flooring, and eating nooks that surrounded everything.

Amy gleamed and lightly touched Ethan's arm. "Wow."

"I know," Ethan said. He smiled at her, happy to have felt her touch, wishing it would last longer.

They were each given plastic cards, an in-house credit card, to charge all of their food on. After they made their rounds, they were to present the card to the cashier.

They waited in line together for their garden salads, then split up. Ethan ordered grilled salmon, shrimp scampi, and mashed potatoes, while Amy picked up fish soup and stuffed bread from the Greek island.

"This is so great," Amy said. She set her tray down on the table Ethan had picked out. Tables were scattered throughout this particular nook, giving each dinner party their own sense of privacy. Ethan and Amy were surrounded by windows and paintings spotlighted by dim lights.

"I cannot believe I got this much food," said Ethan.

"Maybe that's why they give us these plastic cards?"

They both chuckled, agreeing that she had discovered the restaurant's secret to getting their customers to spend more. When they stopped laughing, Amy noticed Ethan looked bewildered.

"What?" she asked.

"What in the world is that?"

Amy smiled. "It's Greek food. I thought I'd be adventurous."

Dinner seemed to last forever. They ate nearly all of their food, saving just enough room for a small, plate-sized chocolate chip cookie, slightly warmed and topped with vanilla ice cream.

As they ate they talked about where they'd gone to college and what they'd been doing since. Amy explained how she'd gone to IUSB, a commuter branch of Indiana University near home. She'd never liked the big school scene. Plus, she had to work at a salon throughout college to be able to afford it. Staying at home and commuting made the most sense to her. She'd worked hard to graduate in four years and was now teaching full time.

Ethan talked of how majoring in mechanical engineering was the only thing that made sense to him. Naturally, he was drawn to Purdue. He explained how he had trouble searching for jobs when he graduated. Nothing seemed to be what he liked or a good fit for him. So he did a search through a website, which landed him a job with the company he ended up working for in Denver. The move was difficult at first, because he'd never been that far away from home, but he got used to it. He loved the mountains, learning to snowboard, and going camping. As time went on he got so bogged down with work that he spent less and less time with the few friends that he had. Finally, he decided it was time to get out and move home.

"Have you figured out how long you're going to be around or what you're going to do next?" asked Amy.

Ethan smiled with his mouth closed, which made his dimples seem even bigger. He'd been waiting for that question.

"I'll be honest, I haven't even looked for another engineering job yet."

"It was that bad, huh?"

He nodded. "I'm not sure what I'm going to do yet. I just want to take some time to be me. You know what I mean?"

"I do."

"Besides, every twenty-six-year-old dreams of moving back in with their parents."

They laughed just loud enough for each other to hear.

Ethan took a drink of water, then cleared his throat. "So what is it about teaching that makes you want to spend all day with those little punks?" asked

Ethan.

"Punks?"

"Let's just say I don't think I'd have the patience for kids."

"Sometimes they can be punks, but overall, they're good." Amy wiped her mouth with her napkin, then set it on top of her plate. "I guess I've always remembered what all of my teachers were like, especially the ones that took extra time to make sure I understood something or gave my best effort. That's what I think about every time I look at those kids, because now I get to be that person. I get to be the one that they will remember for years to come. The teacher that took them aside and made them believe in themselves."

"I'm sure you're good at it too." The sincerity in Ethan's voice made Amy blush.

The date reached the point when it was time to move on. They needed to go someplace new, possibly grab a cup of coffee or go miniature golfing, something to keep the date going. That's when Ethan remembered an article he'd read in the Men's Health magazine Johnny had given him. They said the best thing a man can do on a first date is cut it short. Their hypothesis was that it left the woman wondering how the date had gone, but wanting to spend more time together, leading to another date. The night was going so well that everything inside Ethan was yelling at him to not end the night. Somehow, he resisted.

"Hey I'm glad we were able to have dinner, I've had a great time, but I actually need to be getting back." It was a half-truth anyway; they'd been together for two and a half hours and if they left now it would be half past ten by the time they got home. Ethan needed to open up on Saturday morning, which meant six a.m., though it really didn't matter to him how much sleep he got.

If Amy was surprised she kept herself reserved.

"Oh that's fine." She smiled at Ethan in the same way she had when he first asked her out. "Thank you so much for supper."

Ethan loved it that Amy said the word, "supper." She sounded so cute.

After Ethan paid for their meals and they'd driven back to Amy's apartment, they hugged and said good night.

Just as Amy was about to shut her door, she held it for a moment.

"What are you doing Sunday afternoon?" she asked.

"I don't know, why?"

"Because I'll be at my Grandmother Yoder's house and she's the one that has a copy of the book I want to show you. She lives out on County Line Road. Would you mind coming out there?"

When Ethan heard, "County Line Road," it grabbed his attention. For years, his father had issues with an elderly family with the last name Yoder who lived on that road. Ethan thought to himself, "Could it be the same family?"

He did his best to chase that thought out of his mind, but couldn't. Nonetheless, Ethan was pleasantly surprised and suddenly anxious for Sunday.

CHAPTER 11

Amy's grandmother, Florence Yoder, reminded Ethan of his own grandmother. She walked slowly, with a slight hunch in her back, and spoke with a twang. She had the heart and ambition of a twenty-something stuck in a ninety-two year old body, and no one would ever dare tell her what she could or couldn't do.

Amy and her grandmother had spent the afternoon planting a garden, Florence's favorite hobby. They made even rows of corn, a section for potatoes, green beans, and tomatoes, which were surrounded with wire plant rings. Amy knew that when harvest time came she'd be sitting on the front porch with her mother and her grandmother, canning corn and green beans. Her grandmother took pride in growing her own food and storing it for the winter, just as she used to when she was growing up.

Florence's husband passed away five years ago after a bout with Parkinson's disease. That same disease had claimed Ethan's grandfather. His grandmother passed away just two years ago. Doctors said it was simply because of old age. His mother said it was because of a broken heart. Nonetheless, Ethan tremendously missed having grandparents.

Amy had dirt smeared across her forehead when Ethan stepped out of his truck. She appeared to have gotten into a fight, and quite possibly, could have lost. She looked adorable in her jeans with a hole in the knee and long sleeved fleece.

When Amy introduced Ethan to her grandmother, she looked right into his eyes. "So you are David Miller's son, who was William D. Miller's son, a cousin of Joe Slabach, who was a cousin of my grandfather Gerald Yoder."

Ethan smirked and shook his head from side to side. His grandmother used to do that very same thing. She could recall the family tree of almost anyone around the area and find a way to link that person back to their family. Ethan barely knew his own cousins. Slowly but surely, the older he got the more he learned about his relatives. Yet, he didn't think he'd ever know the tree of people quite like his grandmother did.

Florence looked at Ethan sternly. "Does your father know you're here?" she asked.

Ethan shifted his stance. "No."

"Are you sure you should be here?" She wiped her hands together quickly.

"I don't see why not," he replied.

After that short exchange, Florence showed Ethan to the porch, then went inside. Amy had gone to the bathroom to clean up.

White clouds dotted the endless light blue of the sky. With the light breeze blowing across the porch Ethan felt just right in his long-sleeved T-shirt. The smell of fresh cut grass was all around.

Florence went to the kitchen to wash her hands. She reappeared on the porch wearing an apron that looked as though it had been worn everyday for the past fifty years. She carried a piece of peanut butter pie.

"I brought you some pie." She shut the screen door behind her.

"For me? Are you sure?" He had eaten only an hour ago, but knew if he turned her down that he would offend her.

"I made it this morning." She slid the plate into his hand. "Now take a bite."

He grabbed the fork and took a bite. "It's delicious. Thank you very much."

She smiled and turned around to walk back

inside as though she'd forgotten something.

Ethan swung back and forth on the wooden porch swing while taking one small bite of pie at a time. Whipped cream covered a thick, soft peanut butter fluffed filling. It happened to be one of Ethan's favorites.

It seemed as though five minutes passed before either of them came back outside. Finally, Amy pushed open the screen door. She'd wiped her face clean and had taken off the fleece. She wore a green, short-sleeve T-shirt that read, *Mental Toughness Extra Effort,* with *Cross Country 1998* printed just below. Her hand pressed against his knee as she sat down.

"Grandma will be out in a minute. She's making something to drink."

Ethan placed the fork on his plate. "That sounds perfect. I could use one."

She smiled. "It's a little rich, isn't it?" she asked.

He grinned at her.

A moment later Florence set a cold pitcher of lemonade in front of the three of them, along with three plastic cups. She poured them all a cup, and then told them a story about when she and her husband first moved onto the farm. It originally belonged to her parents, but when they passed away they left it to her. She'd been given a farm with over one hundred acres of green pastures. It was a typical farmhouse, much like all of the others scattered around the outskirts of Middlebury. It had a long dirt lane that lead to a white wooden sided house with an enormous porch on the front of it. Most of the interior had tall and narrow windows, vaulted ceilings, and wide hardwood flooring. There was a red barn with a few cows, a red shed full of tractors and machinery, and a silver silo.

Florence's husband used to be a dairy farmer. He'd milk cows twice a day, at five thirty a.m. and six p.m. She'd been a housewife all her life, raising the children before finally taking care of her husband when he could no longer feed himself. That's what Ethan's grandmother had done too.

Amy placed her right arm behind Ethan, resting it on the top of the backrest of the swing. Her fingertips touched Ethan in the middle of his shoulders.

Florence talked of how her children used to ride horses bareback, how they'd lasso calves, and how one of them had even ridden a bull. As it turned out, that child was Amy's father.

Florence's face came to life when she told a story. Ethan thought it was because she loved having company around and that it was probably something that didn't happen much. That's what had happened to his grandmother anyway.

After Florence had finished with her stories and Amy didn't say anything, Ethan spoke up.

He cleared his throat. "Do you remember my father?" he asked.

Amy placed her hand against Ethan's back and began running her fingertips from side to side. The move surprised Ethan, but he loved how her touch felt. Shivers raced up and down his neck.

Florence looked at Ethan and at her granddaughter. "Of course I do." She peered out at the garden. "He was in my husband's Sunday school class."

Ethan raised his eyebrows. "My dad?"

"The funny thing is I can recall my husband telling me several times how David Miller was such a handful. He used to cause my husband all sorts of problems."

Ethan grinned and shook his head. "Like father, like son."

"He was the ring leader, the leader of all three of those kids in that class. If your father didn't like what was being talked about, none of them did. So my husband's mission was to try to connect with David each Sunday. If he did that, then he felt as though he'd get through to all of them."

Ethan watched Florence rock back and forth in her wooden rocking chair. He noticed how she held a handkerchief in her hands as she talked. She rubbed it with her thumbs as she talked.

"My dad, the troublemaker." Ethan smirked. "I can't say that I'm all that surprised."

Florence crossed her feet. "Boy, was he a handful."

Ethan noticed how quiet things got so quick. He

heard the birds whistling and an engine roar. A truck flew right on past the farm with a thick cloud of dust behind it.

Ethan glanced at Amy, then at Florence. "I don't know what Amy has told you about me, but I'm really curious to find out what happened on Palm Sunday. Do you remember where you were when the tornadoes came through?" he asked.

Without hesitation she said, "I sure do. I was right here, at home."

Ethan noted at the acres of hills that rolled up and down surrounding the farmhouse.

"Come to think of it, I remember a lot about that day. My mother and father had been invited over to what would be your grandparents' house. They had dinner together. I'm sure your father was there." She rocked her chair with a steady pace. She seemed happy with herself for recalling that day so vividly. "My husband and I had come over here in the afternoon to spend time with my parents. My mother and I were taking a walk along the tree line over there." She pointed past the silver silo to a cluster of walnut trees. "We saw a dark sky start to form right in front of our own eyes. It got so dark so quick with clouds piled so high, we didn't know what to think was going on. Then, the winds picked up and things started to get tossed around in the air. My mother and I had to cover our eyes to keep the dirt out of them as we ran for the front door. When my mother tried to pull the door open she couldn't.

At first we thought it was locked, but then she tried again and it budged, so I helped her. It took both of us to open it."

"Why, what happened grandma?" asked Amy.

Florence rubbed her handkerchief with her thumbs. "I don't know, but it was sort of like a vacuum or something. It was as though everything was pressurized. We could barely open the door."

"Did you see a tornado?" Ethan interjected.

Florence eyed both of them. "No, we were miles from anything that touched down, plus we couldn't see over all of those hills." She glanced over the land surrounding them. "Everything blew past us."

Ethan took a deep breath.

Florence looked down at her handkerchief, then into Ethan's eyes. "It's a shame what happened to your father. No one should ever have to go through what he did."

Ethan's stomach tightened. "Can you tell me what happened?"

Florence cleared her throat. "I can tell you what I saw," she said. "My husband and I drove to Middlebury about a half an hour after the big storm passed over here. We figured it was safe then, but we really didn't know. We tried to listen to the radio but none of the stations came in. Nonetheless, we wanted to help whoever we could. One of the first places we stopped was at your grandfather's farm." She blinked, seeming to change the picture in a slide show only she could see. "The house was gone, the barn had been demolished, and the animals were nowhere to be found. Trees had been uprooted, there were piles of wood and debris scattered all over the yard, out in the fields, and across the road. The neighbors place was the same way, nothing was there. Dust filled the air, but the sun was creeping though. Shirts, paper, and random debris was falling from the sky like rain. As we parked the car in your father's dirt lane, we all ran toward the basement of the house, which was the only thing we could tell was still where it was supposed to be. That's when we saw your father. He was lying on his back on the cement floor underneath a few pieces of wooden siding. There weren't any stairs for us to get down there, so my husband lowered himself by holding on to the top of the wall until he could jump. When he got down to your father, he was unconscious."

Florence wiped a teardrop from her cheek.

"Grandma, are you okay?" asked Amy. She leaned forward putting her elbows on her knees.

"Everything was gone." Florence dabbed her eyes with the handkerchief she was holding in her hand. "Your father was seriously hurt."

Ethan hung on every word she said. He couldn't believe what he was hearing.

Florence found Ethan's eyes again. "We sent a neighbor after an ambulance, but none came. There weren't any available. So we took your dad to the hospital in the back of our car. I held him the entire drive. He was lifeless, bleeding out of the back of his head onto me."

Florence folded the handkerchief.

"My husband carried David into the emergency room. I was in awe as we walked in. There must have been a hundred cots lined on both sides of the hall, full of people. They were either still needing to be treated or waiting to be transferred to the Fort Wayne hospital. Almost everyone was covered in soot and mud. I could hardly recognize anyone, but I saw one of my close friends right away. She had a piece of wood through her knee and thigh about a foot long. It looked like someone had stabbed her with a wooden peg."

Florence cleared her throat.

"The entire thing seemed like it wasn't real. We waited and waited for any word on your father. I was asked to help clean cuts and re-dress bandages. Finally, after four hours, we were told your father was going to be okay."

Florence fidgeted with her handkerchief. "I shouldn't be telling you all of this." She stood up, lifted the tray of lemonade and turned toward the screen door.

Ethan leaned forward too, folding his hands. He could see Florence seemed to have become exhausted from reliving her memories of that day. He still had so many questions to ask.

"Grandma, do you want me to get you anything?"

Florence said nothing as she went inside.

Ethan leaned forward, lowered his head, and rubbed the back of his neck with his hand. His time there had come to an end.

Moments later, Ethan asked Amy to thank Florence for her time and the stories. He'd already said good-bye to Amy and started his truck when she came running out to catch him.

"I can't believe I almost let you leave without this." She held up a thin paperback book. It read, *The Darkness of Palm Sunday.*

CHAPTER 12

Later that night, Ethan sprawled out on his bed with his left arm raised behind his head. He stared out his bedroom window trying to digest what he'd just read.

The fifty-page book Amy had given him, took all of forty-five minutes to read. It told the story of the tragic day in much the same way as others had described it. It had been a beautiful day, the morning and afternoon were clear and sunny, but then the skies turned from a baby blue to an eerie yellow to a dark green. Then the unbelievable happened, fifty-one tornadoes moved at a rate of 60

mph, destroying everything. The damage climbed
well over two hundred million dollars, which
merited a visit from President Lyndon B. Johnson.
One tornado covered 273 miles in four hours and
twenty minutes and another was recorded to have
had a base one-mile wide.

Amy's grandfather had also written about a few
specific families. There was a story of an elderly
woman trying to get into her house, but she couldn't
budge her front door open. She struggled with it
right up until the very moment a tornado demolished
it. That tornado even took the very cane she was
leaning on. Somehow, she was left unharmed save
for a scratch on her hand. In another story, a man
hid underneath a wooden table in his basement. The
tornado took his entire house even the foundation of
cement blocks. Yet, the tiny area where he and his
table were at was spared. Even the cardboard boxes
that were sitting on top of the table were still there.
Then there was one family whose house looked like
a giant chainsaw had cut it in two from top to
bottom. Their belongings were scattered across their
yard and into a field. However, there was a set of
drawers neatly stacked on top of each other in the
exact place the desk had been. The drawers still had
the papers piled in order. One gentleman went back
to his home the day after to sort through the
mountain of destruction. Among the debris, he
noticed a book opened to a picture of a tornado,
which caught his eye. It was a book about science,

with an entire section on tornadoes. Below the picture of the tornado were instructions: *Take cover if you ever see a funnel like this. Danger is near*.

Ethan couldn't stop thinking about one account in particular in that book. It was a story about a two-year-old girl, left nameless. She was found lying face down in a cow pasture not more than fifty yards from her home. She still had her Sunday dress on, a barrette in her hair, and black, shiny shoes.

He couldn't stop thinking about how she had done nothing wrong, yet her life was taken away for no reason at all. He kept asking himself, *Isn't there a reason for everything?* He wondered how terrified she must have been and how helpless she felt. *Why was she alone? Why wasn't anyone protecting her?* Her parents must have been devastated.

As his mind continued to wonder, his eyes shifted from the view out the window to the wall beside it. His shelves housed layers of trophies and pictures. He realized he hadn't changed anything about that room since high school, neither had his parents. There were trophies from his little league baseball days when his father coached him to championships. He had pictures of his high school teams, some of Johnny and him and their prom dates, and a few of his parents.

He grabbed the picture of his parents closest to him and leaned back. It happened to be a picture from his high school graduation. Ethan's faced looked narrower and his mother didn't have any gray hairs yet, but his father didn't look any different.

What if, he thought to himself, *What if my parents would have died when I was eighteen? I don't know what I would have done.* He shook his head from side to side, trying to wipe away the thought. He would have missed out on so many little things he often takes for granted. Like how his mother hugs him so tight or the grin his father flashes whenever he's proud. Those are the things that can never be replaced. Those are the things that his father has been without for nearly forty years.

Ethan and David had a good relationship by most standards. They were always there for each other. When Ethan had car trouble, his father helped take care of the problem. When David needed help renovating a room in the house, he always called on Ethan. Through Ethan's baseball playing years David never missed a game, home or away. He wasn't the loudest fan in the stands, but he was there, pacing back and forth by the fence. They were both good at remembering specific games, even certain pitches that Ethan hit for a home run.

Yet, there has always been an invisible wall in between them. Ethan always felt as though his father was holding something back, hiding a part of himself. Now, he was finally beginning to find out why, though he knew he'd never fully know until his father was willing to tell him.

Knock, knock, knock.

"Someone's here to see you," his mother said.

Ethan sat up, placed the picture back in its spot on the shelf and walked toward the door. "All right, I'm coming."

His mother headed down the stairs as he opened the door. He trailed behind her. At the bottom of the stairs was the front door, slung open, with Amy standing there smiling on the front porch. When Ethan finally stood in front of her, he realized he couldn't remember walking down the stairs.

"What are you doing here?" he asked. He leaned in to give her a quick hug. She hugged him back. "Well, I was in the neighborhood." She tilted her head and smiled.

"Uh huh," he said, studying her.

Amy shifted her weight, then stood up straight. "Actually, I was sort of wondering if you'd like to go do something."

She smiled, the flash of white from her teeth matching the cotton T-shirt she wore beneath her jean jacket.

Fireworks went off in Ethan's stomach. "You bet. Let me slip on some shoes."

He knelt down by the pile of shoes beside the door. Ethan tried to hurry and leave before his parents demanded to meet Amy. Out of the corner of his eye, he saw his mother and father walking closer.

"Will you tell your mother we said hi?" asked Jeanne.

"I will," said Amy.

Ethan looked up. "I take it you've all met?" He struggled fiercely to get his right shoe on.

"About two minutes ago," said David. "As it turns out we know her family."

"Oh, I see." said Ethan. He grabbed his coat off the tree stand. "See ya," he said, and then closed the door. He knew he'd have some explaining to do when he got home. Her family was the Yoder family Ethan's father had issues with.

In an attempt to clear his mind, Ethan whispered to Amy, "Stalker."

Amy furrowed her brow. "What?"

Ethan threw on his jacket. "How'd you know where I lived?"

"My mom knew, of course. She knows where everyone lives." Amy winked. "It's a side project of hers."

Satisfied, Ethan smiled. "So where are we going?"

"I'm feeling outdoorsy. What if we make a fire?" asked Amy. The night felt slightly cool, but warm enough to be outside. "I've got blankets in the back of my Honda and I know of a perfect place that's got wood and a fire pit already set up."

"Where's that?"

"One of my grandmother's fields."

The thought of holding Amy close was all the motivation he needed. "You know what, let's do it. Sounds great."

Fifteen minutes later, back a dark trail and into

an open section of woods, Amy and Ethan removed logs from a stack of dried wood and set them in the fire pit like a teepee. After spritzing the wood with lighter fluid, Amy tossed in a match and the fire took off in a hurry.

Ethan and Amy leaned against a log sitting on one blanket with another draped over their shoulders. At first they just sat close to each other, but soon Ethan raised his arm around Amy's shoulders and she slid into him.

Ethan cleared his throat. "So, what made you track me down tonight?" he asked.

Amy re-situated herself slightly. "I don't know what it was exactly, but we didn't get much time to talk earlier today."

Not exactly the answer he was hoping for.

She continued, "And plus, I wanted to see you." Then she leaned her head on his chest.

Thank you, Johnny, and thank you, Men's Health, he thought to himself. Only two days ago they'd had their first date and now he was snuggling with someone he could see a future with. Things were good.

"I hope that was okay?" she asked.

"This is about the best way I can see spending my evening," he said.

Over the next hour, Ethan tossed in three more logs as they talked about living in Indiana - what they liked about it and what they didn't. They agreed that family was extremely important to both

of them and that it was the biggest reason they lived
there now. They talked about the different seasons
and how Indiana seems to get each of them to the
fullest: the winter brings in lake effect snow off
Lake Michigan and dumps it without notice; the rain
doesn't stop for most of spring; the heat and
humidity of the summer is reminiscent of the south;
and the leaves are a perfect yellow, orange, and red
every fall. But they agreed that one of the best
things about living in this town was the stars,
especially on a night like tonight.

"Do you know the names of any constellations?"
asked Amy.

"You mean other than the Big Dipper?"

"Yep," she said as she nudged him.

"Then, no."

"Me neither. That's sad." They laughed in
unison.

Then they both fell silent, shifting their eyes
back and forth from the flame of the fire to the crisp
stars above them. Ethan could see the top of Amy's
forehead as he looked down at her. He wondered
what she was thinking.

Was it time? Should he go for it? He was never
good at this. *The night seemed perfect, and she
seemed perfect. Wouldn't a kiss seal it all?*

He lowered his head slightly, wondering if she
noticed. Pausing for a moment, he snuck a glimpse
at her again, and then kissed her forehead. She
slowly lifted her head toward his. The touch of her

lips on his cheek sent chills through the back of his neck. When their lips finally met, Ethan's insides did somersaults against his stomach. He had completely fallen for Amy. They kissed slowly until only a red glow from the coals of the fire was left.

CHAPTER 13

"Dad, are you ready?" asked Ethan.

It was Wednesday evening and Amy's grandmother, Florence, called to see if Ethan could bring his father to her house. When Ethan talked to her on the telephone, she wasn't willing to say any more than that, but was adamant they come over.

After convincing David to get in his truck, Ethan turned the radio to the Chicago Cubs baseball game. When his father asked him where they were going, he brushed it off saying, "You'll see." He searched for conversation, but couldn't come up with anything.

The drive took them through Middlebury, past Sturdy Oak Park, then Ivan's Ice Cream Shoppe, followed by the one stoplight in town. Ethan noticed that all of the trees and the branches hanging over the road were leafless and identically brown, making the drive seem longer than it was. A couple of dairy farms later, Ethan turned left, onto County Line Road.

Ethan's heart pounded as hard and loud as a bass drum. Pulling into Florence's dirt lane, he caught a glimpse of his father's clenched jaw. He never told his parents that he'd been there, until now.

David smacked the dashboard. "You what?"

"Dad, chill out. I was over here on Sunday afternoon." Ethan went on to explain how Amy had invited him over to her grandmother's house.

Ethan recognized the tilt of his father's head, and the glare of his eyes, as the, *you've been up to something and I know I won't like it* look. The wrinkles that had spread from the corner of David's eyes were as detailed as a road map.

The vein in David's forehead looked as though it could explode at any moment. He aimed his voice directly into Ethan's right ear, "But why would she do that and why would you go along with it?"

Ethan explained how he'd seen the article in the newspaper about the tornado. He said how he talked with Amy about it briefly at the coffee shop and she mentioned that her grandfather had written a book about the tornadoes. Then he told him about their date and how they had such a good time that she invited him over to her grandmother's house to pick up the book. He also mentioned that he'd read the book.

Ethan could almost see steam coming out of his father's ears. He hadn't said a word since Ethan started talking.

Florence stood in front of the screen door. She waved, motioning them in as the truck came to a halt. Then she disappeared back inside.

Ethan got out, shut the door, and began walking toward the porch. He took three steps before he noticed his father hadn't moved.

"Come on, Dad," he said. His voice remained calm, hoping to ease the obvious tension his father had built up. Still, he didn't budge. Instead, he seemed only more enraged. David's face looked flushed, his jaw tight, and the door locked.

Ethan walked back to his window and twirled his hand, asking his father to lower it.

His father snapped his head at him. "I'm not going in there!"

Ethan bunched his eyebrows, wrinkling his forehead. "Dad, she just wants to show you something." He paused, "That's it, then we're out of here."

David looked the other way, then took a deep breath. "You don't even know what you're doing." He climbed out and slammed the door behind him.

They walked toward the front porch steps,

neither saying a word. When they reached the
screen door, Florence appeared on the other side.

She held open the door. "I'm glad you boys
could make it."

Ethan smiled and led the way in. David
managed to nod as he entered. Florence took them
into the living room, and then offered some
lemonade to drink. Neither of them took her up on
her offer. The smell of tea leaves permeated the air.
Ethan and his father sat on a tan couch with buttons
that created divots every six inches. Across the
room sat a wood-burning stove with a kettle of water
on top. To the right of that stood a bookshelf, filled
with books on all three levels. An aloe vera plant sat
directly beside a radio with a broken antenna on top
of the bookshelf. A static version of jazz played out
of yellow mesh speakers.

Ethan noticed Florence looked anxious,
fidgeting with the handkerchief she held in her
hands. She kept folding and unfolding it. She also
kept biting her lip. The silence was nearly
unbearable. He questioned whether this was a good
idea or not.

"David, it's nice to see you again." She paused,
taking a deep breath. "I know you didn't want to
come here, but thank you." She sighed.

David didn't look at her. He rubbed the back of
his neck and pressed his lips together.

"I'll get right to the reason you're here." She
scooted to the edge of the yellow, brown, and green

striped wingback chair she was seated on. "I've
been meaning to share something with you for a
long time." She looked down at the handkerchief as
she folded it again. "After seeing Ethan, I knew I
had do this now, even though I should have years
ago."

She began. "After you left, Ethan, I got to
thinking about April 11, 1965." She paused, waiting
for David to look at her, which he didn't. "I still feel
as though it was all yesterday. And David, I've
thought about you over the years more than you'll
know. You've been in my prayers."

David nodded, blinking his eyes slowly.

The room fell quiet again. Only the fuzzy sound
of jazz could be heard. Ethan saw his father looking
down at the faded green carpet. His arms were
folded across his chest. Ethan noticed Florence
meddling with her handkerchief again. Her eyes
made their way to Ethan. He nodded for her to
continue.

"I'm sorry that you didn't like what was said in
that book," said Florence. She peered at David,
pleading. "I'd take it all back if I could." Her eyes
became glassy.

David continued to stare at the carpet, his jaw
clenched. He shook his head from side to side, then
quickly looked up at her. "Florence, is this the
reason you wanted us to come over here?"

She pulled herself up out of the chair by the
armrest, and then motioned for them to follow her.

The three of them climbed up a staircase stained a dark cherry, with steps nearly six feet wide, and an oversized handrail, which Florence gripped tightly. She led them into a storage room with walls halfway paneled and half exposed, revealing wooden siding, the outside of the house. Spider webs and dust covered everything. It appeared as though no one had been in that room for years.

Florence maneuvered her way to the very back corner of the room where she pulled a tablecloth off of some sort of chest. Straps of leather wrapped around the wooden box holding it closed. A lock clasped the lid shut on the front of it. She turned, facing Ethan and David.

"I need one of you boys to break this off." She pointed to the lock. "I have no idea where the key is."

Ethan knelt down, analyzing the lock. It appeared to be in great condition considering he didn't know how old it was. "Do you have a crowbar or hammer or anything like that?"

Florence paused for a moment. "I think those things are all out in the shed. Would you mind running and getting whatever you need?"

Ethan left his father and Florence all alone in that tiny room. He figured Florence would try to strike up some kind of conversation with his father again. That would probably be useless. Ethan couldn't figure out why his father was so ticked off to be here. He'd never seen him act this way.

Ethan wiped his brow. He'd returned, sweaty
and out of breath. The air felt heavy in that room,
just like on a hot, humid day. He saw Florence
peering out the window. Her white, lace lined apron
covered the miniature interlinked roses that traveled
up and down her dress. He noticed her shoes were
plain black with a strap tucked into a gold buckle
across the top.

Ethan held a crowbar in his left hand and a
hammer in his right. He handed both of them to his
father.

David wedged the crowbar in between the lock
and the opening of the trunk. He pushed against the
crowbar, tried to yank it a few times, and nothing
happened. Then he tried a different angle, grabbed
the hammer, and swung.

Clank.

The lock snapped and fell to the floor. David
took a step back.

Florence reached out and wiped her hand across
the top of the trunk. "This has been sitting here for
almost forty years," she said. Her filled with water.

She continued, "I've never seen what's inside of
it." Her hands quivered back and forth. Then she
turned and looked for David's again. "This is why
you are here."

David rubbed the back of his neck again.

Ethan leaned against the doorway, listening
intently.

"David, I know you saw things in a way that no

one else did that day. Only you know what you've had to go through over the years. But if it wasn't for my father, I don't know if you'd be alive."

"I know," he said. He finally looked her in the eyes.

"The day after the tornado went through my father went out to try to help salvage anything he could." She wiped a tear from the corner of her eye. "He found some things and he put them in here. I remember him saying that he wanted to find the people who would know what they were, but it was too difficult to talk about. He died shortly thereafter and this has been sitting here ever since."

David's cheeks took on a bright red color. His eyes widened.

"I had forgotten about it until Ethan came over." She put her hand on David's left arm. "I want you to open that."

David swallowed, which looked like a difficult thing to do at the moment. He stepped closer and placed both of his hands on the corners of the trunk. Then he took a deep breath and slowly lifted the lid.

A cloud of dust quickly rose out of nowhere. The hinges squeaked.

Hunched over, David could see blankets and a couple of shirts, all perfectly folded. He began taking off a layer at a time and setting them on the floor beside him. There was a yearbook from Topeka High School, an unscratched 8 x 10 of a family he'd never seen before, and a letter jacket.

David cleared his throat. "These are all people's personal things."

He held up the yearbook.

Florence dabbed the corners of her eyes with her handkerchief and nodded.

As David placed the letter jacket on the floor beside him, he paused for a moment. He reached back in the trunk, digging down farther. Then he pulled out a shoe, staring at it as though he'd seen a ghost. It was a black flat with a strap that looped through a gold buckle. He quickly leaned back over the trunk sifting through the things. He suddenly stopped.

Ethan walked closer. "Dad, what is it?"

David slowly lowered himself to his knees, then leaned against the trunk with his arms spread out over it. His body began to shake as though he was convulsing.

Ethan placed his hand in the middle of his father's back and leaned down beside him. "Dad, what is it?" he asked again.

David's body shook from trying to hold in his tears. Ethan held out his arms, embracing him.

Florence leaned against the wall watching as tears streamed down her cheeks.

Finally, David looked at Ethan. His eyes were red, his cheeks flooded. He reached in the chest and pulled out two black, shiny shoes and placed them in Ethan's open hands.

"These were your grandmother's." David said.

Ethan looked down at them in awe.

Then David reached back into the trunk and pulled out a leather book. It had a leather strap that clasped, holding the book shut. He held it in his hands, staring at it.

"And this was your grandfather's."

He set the journal on the ground in front of him and reached back into the trunk. He paused, convulsing, fighting his tears back. Then he pulled out a well-worn fuzzy bear with a heart sewn on its chest.

CHAPTER 14

David looked mesmerized, staring into a candle's flame. He watched as it grew tall, reaching high, barely moving. Then it would fall short, flickering to stay lit as though it were going to give up. Over the past hour, it still hadn't blown out.

He had plopped down in the recliner with his feet up, debating what he should do. On top of his lap sat his father's leather journal. It had been two days since he'd found it, yet he hadn't been able to get himself to open it.

As soon as he saw it in the trunk, he immediately relived memories of his father seated in

his favorite chair with this journal in his hands.
Even as David held it now, he could still see his
father gazing out the living room window sifting
through his thoughts, writing them out on the very
pages concealed within that leather cover. That's
why David hadn't been able to open it. He kept
wrestling with whether this was invading his father's
privacy or not.

   David walked to the kitchen, poured himself
another glass of water, then returned to the recliner.
Jeanne was on the couch reading the latest Oprah
Book Club novel. She usually cruised through a
book a week. Typical nights around that house
found her reading while David watched "Seinfeld"
re-runs or the local news.

   When David and Ethan came back from
Florence's place, both of them looked as though
they'd put in a full day of farming. Ethan set the
pair of shoes on the kitchen table, got a glass of
water, and went upstairs to his bedroom. David sat
down at the table, in front of the shoes. He didn't
speak for a moment, which must have seemed like
an hour to Jeanne. Undoubtedly, she had a number
of questions that needed answered. Finally, David
handed the teddy bear to her. Then he told her what
they'd found up in Florence's attic. Jeanne cried.

   The three of them had been quiet around each
other ever since. Ethan figured his father was still
upset with him for nosing around. Yet, he knew if
he hadn't done that, then odds were his father would

have never known any of those things existed.
Ethan still had no idea why the teddy bear was so
important. David wasn't sure what to say to anyone.
He was just trying to let everything sink in. Jeanne
was the only one who seemed normal, but she didn't
want to ask anything that David or Ethan weren't
ready to talk about. So she hadn't spoken much
either.

David set his glass of water down beside the
candle and picked up the book. He pressed two
buttons that released the leather strap holding the
journal closed and opened it. The binding felt stiff,
making David hold the cover so it would stay open.
In the upper left hand corner his father had written
his name: *William D. Miller.* David ran his finger
over the name as he envisioned his father writing it.

The pages were warped and dried as though
they'd once been wet. The first page crinkled like a
dried out fallen leaf as he turned it. The ink had
faded slightly, but the words were manageable
although the penmanship was close to a doctor's
scribble. David began to read the first entry.

> *January 4, 1943*
> *I turned eighteen today and my father*
> *gave me this journal. I'm not very good at*
> *writing. I don't know what to write about.*
> *I will try again tomorrow.*
>
> *William*

David analyzed the handwriting of his father almost as though looking for some hidden clue. All of his thoughts were written in ink, so there wasn't a possibility of erasing and writing them over. Everything down on those pages was authentic, straight from his father's heart.

As David read through the first few entries he noted that his father had written off and on, about once a month, for the first year. They were short paragraphs about what he'd done that specific day: how he'd gotten a job at the mill and was no longer working in the fields, the times he'd been fishing and how many he'd caught, and the girls he'd seen and those he hoped yet to meet.

As he turned yet another page of the diary, he felt something slide out from the back. He moved his finger to that page and opened it. In that moment, he no longer heard the tick of the grandfather clock across the room. He took the object out and set the book down. He grinned as he ran his fingertips over the object.

David walked over and sat beside Jeanne on the couch. His eyes were wide as though smiling themselves.

"Honey, you won't believe what this is." He held up a square piece of paper. As he flipped it around, Jeanne saw a black and white photo. It had a tear in the bottom right corner, but the photo was still crisp. Her eyes scanned the faces. It was David's family.

She did a double take. "Oh my goodness!" she exclaimed.

He handed her the photo. She pulled it close seeing how much David's younger face looked like Ethan's.

David shook his head. "I think that was the last family photo we ever took."

Jeanne couldn't stop smiling. She hugged David, then handed him the photo.

Back in his seat, David touched the faces on the picture, wishing they were real. He remembered when they took that picture. It was at the church on one of the most humid days of the summer. His mother had griped about her hair looking like a big curly mess. She had natural curls that bounced when she walked, but they also made her grit her teeth whenever she tried to comb them. However, there was one thing missing from that picture that made David feel empty inside. Rebecca wasn't in it. She hadn't been born yet.

David carefully placed the picture on top of the end table and picked up the leather journal again. Over the course of an hour David had learned so much about his father that his childhood seemed more real and closer than it had in years.

The candle still flickered back and forth as David turned to the entry he'd left off at.

June 19, 1945

Sometimes I wonder why I even write in here, but tonight I'm glad I do because I just had the best night of my life and I've got to tell someone about it.

In my family we have a tradition that the father has to talk to his son about specific things in life. A year ago, my father and I had that very talk. He talked about sex, money, and what it means to be the leader of a household. I just listened.

The very last thing we talked about was love. He asked me what love was. I tried to tell him, but nothing I said made sense. My father went on to explain that I need to think about what it means to love someone. He said that my future wife will not only depend on me telling her of my love for her, but that I will also need to show her, and hold her needs up above my own. He said that when I met the right woman that I would come to the realization on my own that love is something so precious and beautiful that it is worth believing in. That's when he asked me if I would carry on the Miller family tradition. My father asked me if I would write a letter to my future wife describing the love that I believe in and that I want to share with her one day.

> *That very night, I did just that. It took
> me all night, but I did it. I wrote a letter to
> my future wife.*
>   *He was right. I did discover how
> precious and beautiful love is when you find
> the right woman. Her name is Miriam.
> Tonight, I watched as she cried when she
> read the letter that I had written for her
> before we'd ever met.*
>   *Then, I proposed to her.
> She said yes.*
>
>   *William*

David set the leather bound journal in his lap.
He leaned back in his recliner and put his hands on
his head. His stomach felt nauseous and his heart
heavy. His father never had that talk with him.
David didn't even know it, but he'd broken the
family tradition. It was just one of the millions of
things he'd been stripped of over the years.

David clasped shut the leather bound journal and
set it on the end table. He blew out the candle,
stretched, and then walked toward the stairway.

Jeanne looked up. "Honey, are you going to
bed?" she asked.

He gave her a tip of the hat salute as he
continued onward. "Right after I hit the bathroom,"
he said.

David figured Jeanne was probably going nuts,
eyeing the leather cover, wondering what was

written on those pages. He hadn't let her read any of it nor had he told her what he'd read so far. She could easily sneak a peak without him knowing. He stopped in mid stride and nearly turned around. He trusted her though, so he let it be. She knew how important that leather journal was to him. Besides, that clasp wasn't the easiest thing to open, especially for someone with nails.

That night David rolled from side to side in bed. His eyes were closed but his body wouldn't fall asleep. Life wasn't fair. He couldn't stop thinking about the father-son talk that was supposed to have happened, the family tradition, and Jeanne.

If his father had given him that talk, would he have made some different decisions along the way? Did he do things right? What would his father say about his life? Would he be proud? What would he have written in that letter to his future wife? Did he and Jeanne make the right decision to get married? Did they rush into it? Has he given her the love she had dreamt of?

They'd had their share of rocky waves, with all of his job changes and money being tight. She'd never doubted him though, and he knew it.

David rolled on his side again, this time facing Jeanne. She was in a deep sleep, breathing heavily through her nose. The moonlight fell through the window casting shadows across her face. They followed each curve, lying wherever they wanted to. He touched his fingertips to her forehead. Then he slowly traveled the bridge of her nose, to her lips, around her jaw, and back to where he started. Her skin felt as soft as velvet. Even after forty years of marriage, she still resembled the beauty she was in high school. There were, of course, changes. He'd seen her hair transform from brown, to blonde, to red, and now, light brown again. Her once-faint dimple is now more prevalent than ever. Yet, she still didn't need any makeup to look amazing. David traced her face, feeling as close to her as those shadows.

He kissed her on the cheek and whispered, "I love you."

CHAPTER 15

Ethan watched as shadows danced across Amy's face. They were cast from the dim light sitting on the corner of their table. As she smiled, they smiled. As she laughed, they laughed. And as she stopped to look at him, they stopped to look too.

They were alone at the coffee shop. Ethan had been asked to work the night shift on Friday, which meant cleaning everything and prepping for the following day. On Wednesday morning, Amy had volunteered to help, or at least hang out while he finished up whatever it was he had to do. After the dishes had been washed and the espresso machines cleaned, they were listening to the soothing jazz of Norah Jones and playing a game of checkers on a table with an oversized checkerboard painted on it.

The anticipation of being close to Amy again had been building up in Ethan's mind the entire week. The only times they'd seen each other since they'd kissed were in the morning when Amy made her usual latte stop. She had parent-teacher conferences all week, so her evenings were tied up, and when she wasn't busy she said she was too exhausted.

Ethan told her how her grandmother invited his father and him over. He unraveled the story of how they'd discovered the diary, a pair of shoes, and a mysterious teddy bear, in some trunk in a storage room. Her lips parted in astonishment. She didn't breathe until Ethan finished with his story. She told Ethan how weird it made her feel to think back to all of those times she and her cousins had been in that room toying with that lock. They were beside a treasure chest. Her eyes watered up as Ethan told how his father had been reading through the diary and the way he had smiled as he showed him the picture of his family.

When Amy asked him what her grandmother was going to do with the other things in the trunk, he threw his hands into the air. He and his father left too quickly to ask any questions.

Amy leaned against the wall sitting on one leg, staring off into nowhere. The checkers game had ended, Ethan had gotten everything ready for the morning crew, and it was closing in on midnight. Time had once again slid through Ethan's fingers. He wanted more of it. If he could just find more time to be with Amy, then maybe he could see where this was going.

There was something comforting about Amy. Ethan could talk to her about anything. She always listened, asked questions, and wanted to know everything, plus she knew all about the tornado and why it had become so important to Ethan.

As Amy repositioned herself, the shadows now draped from her cheekbone. Her skin looked smooth and Ethan wanted to be next to it again. The music was right. The mood was perfect.

Just ask her to dance.

No one else was around. Ethan's heart began picking up pace as he counted the moments passing that he'd wasted.

She'll think it's a stupid idea.

Ethan had noted to himself that they hadn't kissed at all, let alone touched hands since they'd hugged when she first walked in.

Maybe she's not as interested as I am? What if this is just a friend thing to her? What about the kiss though?

As Ethan battled his thoughts Amy shifted in her seat and turned her eyes back on Ethan.

Just do it, ask her to dance. Take a chance. Put your heart out there. She's worth it.

"Have you ever played shuffleboard?" she asked.

Ethan tilted his head. *Did she just say that?* "You mean the game most retired people in Florida play?"

Amy chuckled. "No, no. But it's close to that."

Ethan grinned. "Then I have no idea what you are talking about."

Amy stood up. "All right, let's go."

She smiled and walked toward the door. Ethan turned out the lights and locked the coffee shop. Amy waited, facing the direction they would be walking. She mentioned that a fierce game of shuffleboard would be played out momentarily at The Corner Pocket. He knew the place she was talking about. He and Johnny had been there a few times to play pool.

"Did I tell you that this coming week is my spring break?" asked Amy.

Ethan's stomach sank. "I don't think so."

"No kids, no grading papers, I don't have much to do at all so I'm going to Florida." Amy gleamed. For some reason, the place for people from Indiana to go on vacation has typically been Florida. When Ethan was in high school, that's where he and his friends went on their spring breaks. And the only family vacation he and his parents ever took was down there too.

"That's not fair, is it?" he asked.

"Of course it is. I deserve it."

"You do." But Ethan only thought about how he'd have to go an entire week without seeing her. Considering they'd only just begun to get to know each other, he couldn't believe how disappointed he felt.

Two blocks later, Amy and Ethan stopped underneath a neon green sign that read, The Corner Pocket, in cursive. Ethan pulled the door open and held it as Amy walked through. The Corner Pocket looked narrow, but long. A U-shaped bar stood out at the entrance of the pub. In the back were ten pool tables, along with a haze of smoke hovering over the crowd of people playing pool. Everything seemed to have been recently renovated. New carpet, shiny bar, and sports games were playing on all of the televisions that hung from the ceiling.

"Hey Stan." Amy spoke to the bartender as though they were long time friends.

"Hey trouble. Back again, huh?"

"You bet. I've got to keep my winning streak alive."

Stan reached underneath the counter, pulled out a tiny box, and handed it to Amy. He looked at Ethan.

"Good luck. She's ruthless."

Ethan grinned. "Thanks."

"There it is." Amy pointed to a long table pushed up against the wall. It looked about thirty feet long and three feet wide. The middle of the table was made of hardwood, reminiscent of a basketball floor. A thin layer of sand stretched across the entire surface. A four inch wide carpeted trough surrounded the hardwood, making a ledge for the pucks to fall into.

"So that's what that is?" Ethan pointed to the table, touching the sand on the surface. "Every time I come here I see that thing and wonder what in the world it is."

Amy grinned. "Now you know."

She opened the box and set eight silver pucks on the table. "Okay, the object of the game is to push this little puck down to the other end and get it to stop on a number."

There were triangles painted on both ends of the table that read "1,2,3,4."

Ethan pulled a bar stool near the table. "That's it?" he asked as he perched on top of the seat.

Amy smirked. "Yep, that's it. However, I will tell you it's not as easy as it looks. The sand makes it really slick."

She separated the pucks into two piles of four. The pucks were slightly larger than a half-dollar coin and were either blue or red in the middle.

"I'll be the red ones and you be the blue. The first one to ten wins."

Ethan nodded. "Sounds good."

Amy stepped closer to the end of the shuffleboard, steadied herself, and pushed the first puck toward the other end. It glided slowly to the other end where it came to a stop on the number three.

"Nice shot."

Amy winked. "Thanks, your turn."

Ethan hopped off the seat and placed his left hand on the table. He gripped the puck in his right hand, pushed, and watched it glide twice as fast as Amy's had. The puck fell into the gully at the end of the table.

Ethan shook his head from side to side. "Whoops."

"Not so fast, Mr. Muscles." She said.

Amy placed her hand in the middle of Ethan's back as she made her way to the table again. A cool shiver raced up and down his spine. The magic of her touch made him wish he knew her better than he did.

Amy situated herself to push the next puck. "Now take notes on the technique. You have to sway back and forth a little to control the speed of the puck." She smiled. "Watch."

She swayed slightly back and forth and released the puck. It glided across the sand stopping next to her first toss on the number three.

Ethan flashed his dimples at her. "Okay, so I see you have obviously played this a few times."

Amy grinned. "I guess you can say that."

Ethan motioned for her to have a seat on the chair. "How many times have you played?"

Amy sat down. "Just a few. We have a group of teachers that go out once in a while. This is where we end up."

Ethan picked up his next puck. "Uh huh. Why do I feel like I'm getting hustled?" He took his position at the end of the table.

Ethan glanced at Amy. "So tell me something about you."

Amy crossed her legs. "Well what do you want to know?"

He glanced at her, catching those familiar green eyes he'd memorized. "Anything. Tell me something I don't know about you."

Ethan steadied himself, swayed his body a bit, then released the puck. It glided slowly down toward the other end. It nearly stopped on the four, but toppled over the edge, again landing in the gully.

"I once had a frog climb up my pants," Amy said. She laughed as she heard those words come out.

"What?" he asked. Ethan smiled and stepped back from the table.

Amy hopped off the chair. "I think I might have been seven or eight. My parents and I were coming back from dinner with another family. I was walking in from the car. When I got to the door, I felt something on my shin, shimmying its way up my leg. So I started to jump around." She smirked.

"I'll bet you did." Ethan placed his hand on the small of her back as she passed by. He looked in her eyes.

Amy stopped where she was and used her hands to help explain her story. "The next thing I knew, I was standing in front of everyone in my underwear as they were all trying to catch the leaping frog. It was hysterical."

They laughed together. Ethan pulled his hand away as she got ready for her next shot.

"That's funny." Ethan stood behind the stool, put his hands down on top of it, and leaned forward.

Amy readied herself. "Your turn," she said.

Ethan looked down at the ground, then up at her. "When I was about the same age, I told my dad I was leaving."

Amy glanced at Ethan, grinning. "What?"

Ethan laughed under his breath. "Yeah, I told my dad I didn't want to go to school anymore and that I was running away. So, I packed a duffle bag with some t-shirts and shorts, said goodbye, and started walking." Ethan shifted his weight back and forth. "I must have been a half mile down the road before my dad took me serious."

Amy shook her head from side to side.

"I probably would have kept walking if he hadn't come after me. He ended up walking with me for a little while, before convincing me to come home."

Ethan watched Amy, as her eyes followed his. They were on the same page. He knew right then, he wanted to kiss her again.

"Guess what?" asked Amy.

Ethan raised his eyebrows. "What?"

"I just won." Amy smiled.

You won more than the game, Ethan thought to himself. *You just won my heart.*

CHAPTER 16

Johnny was late and Ethan was ticked. It was Wednesday night and he was sitting atop a barstool at The Corner Pocket watching ESPN highlights. After Ethan mentioned to Johnny that he had played shuffleboard with Amy at The Corner Pocket, Johnny thought it would be fun to shoot some pool. He also said he'd be there at eight. It was half past, and he still hadn't walked through the front door.

The Corner Pocket had foot rails of shiny brass, tall and padded bar stools, and six television sets that crowded the wall behind the bar, all showing sports. Ethan had never sat at a bar by himself before and

felt a like he'd been transported to a foreign land.
His ears were burning as though people were talking
about him, wondering what he was doing. He'd told
the bartender he was waiting for a friend, but felt
like an idiot sitting there without ordering anything.
When he asked for a Hornsby, the bartender said
he'd never heard of it, so he'd been nursing a beer
and tossing peanut after peanut into his mouth.

"Is that Ethan? Ethan Miller?" A soft voice
asked.

He turned around. His neck extended and his
eyebrows lifted. Of all people, it was Melinda Lane.

"Melinda?" She still looked wonderful with her
sandy brown hair, eyes the color of coffee, and lips
full like Angelina Jolie's. That's what he'd always
remember about Melinda.

She leaned in toward him. "Oh my goodness,"
she said. They hugged quickly, and then she stepped
back.

"I haven't seen you in," he looked toward the
ground, and then back up at her, "what, five or six
years?"

"I think so."

"What are you doing here?" he asked. "I heard
you moved to Chicago."

"I did actually." She shifted her stance. "Here's
the short version." She smiled and drew in a deep
breath. "I went to Northwestern, then got married,
worked as a nurse at General, had a kid, and then got

divorced. Now I'm back in the area. I just started working at Memorial Hospital."

Ethan offered a friendly smile as though to say that he understood.

"Well it's good to see you," he said.

"What about you?"

"I'll give you the short version too." He grinned. "I went to Purdue, was an engineer in Denver, never got married. Now, I live at home and serve coffee at One More Cup." Ethan exhaled as though amused by his own life.

"You lived in Denver?" she asked.

"Well, well, well." Johnny had walked right into the conversation without either of them noticing. "If this isn't a reunion I don't know what is."

Johnny and Melinda greeted each other, hugged, then stepped back. She gave him the very same short version she'd given Ethan. Johnny updated her too. Then an awkward pause in conversation slid in between them.

"So what are you doing here?" asked Johnny.

"I'm supposed to meet a friend for a game of pool. I think I'm a little early," said Melinda.

"Imagine that," Ethan barked at Johnny, "being early for something when you don't have to."

"Sorry man, the wife was giving me a hard time about going out." Johnny pleaded. "You're lucky I'm here."

"I guess so."

Melinda eyed the door. "There she is," she said. All three of them looked in that direction. It was a face unfamiliar to both Ethan and Johnny.

After the women said hello to each other, Melinda turned facing them again. "This is Elizabeth, she was my college roommate and is in town from Chicago." She paused. "And this is Ethan," she said as she pointed at him, "and this is Johnny."

When they'd all smiled at each other, Johnny asked, "Would you two like to join us in a game of pool?"

Melinda's forehead wrinkled as she looked at Elizabeth. Then she turned back toward Johnny, "I think we're just going to have a couple of drinks for now. We might take you up on that later though."

"Okay. Well it was great to see you, Melinda, and nice to meet you Elizabeth." He sounded smooth. Johnny had always been comfortable around women. Ethan said nearly the same thing to them, then led the way to the pool table.

Ethan smiled and shook his head as he put all of the pool balls in their correct spot in the triangle.

"What are you grinning about?" asked Johnny.

Ethan looked up at him. "Oh, you and your way with women."

Johnny threw his hands up. "Now what did I do?"

Ethan grabbed a pool stick and started chalking the end of it. "Nothing, it's just the way you say things sometimes. It's like you're flirting with them even when you aren't."

Johnny put his hands on the ledge of the pool table and leaned on it. "It's a gift, I know." He winked at Ethan. "Don't give up yet. You'll get there too if you keep working at it."

Ethan eyed Johnny. "Why don't you go ahead and break first?"

Over the next hour they played four games of pool and jumped from conversations about the Cubs and how they thought they'd do in the upcoming season, to work, to when they were going golfing next, and finally to women. Everything always came back to women.

"So what's up with this Amy girl?" asked Johnny.

Ethan eyed his next shot, lining the cue stick up perfectly. "I don't know what's going on with her yet."

Johnny smirked. "You don't?"

"Nope." Ethan slowly pulled the cue stick back, then shot it forward. His stick struck the cue ball, which bounced off the five ball, and glanced off both edges of the hole.

"Well you need to put on some man pants and find out," said Johnny.

Ethan chuckled to himself.

"I think things are good, but we haven't talked about a relationship or anything remotely close to that." He stood tall, holding his cue stick. "Besides, she's young and I don't think there's any need to rush things."

Johnny leaned over the pool table preparing for his next shot. "All right, fair enough." He sank his shot and walked around to the other side of the table to ready himself again. "But, you're not getting any younger are you?"

Ethan took the end of his cue stick and smacked Johnny on the hamstring.

"Ouch." Johnny eyed Ethan.

"Not all of us can have everything work out just like we want it to," Ethan said with a sharp tone.

"Yeah." Johnny nodded. "You're absolutely right. My marriage is like the perfect ending to a movie." Johnny smirked. "You've got no idea what it takes to make a marriage work."

"You're right," Ethan snapped back. "I don't."

"Take tonight for instance." Johnny took a step back, eyed his next shot. "When I mentioned to Brooke that I wanted to hang out with you for a couple of hours tonight, she gave me the eye of betrayal."

Ethan shook his head from side to side. "Why?"

"I don't know." Johnny leaned close to his pool stick, readying himself. "I think sometimes she expects me to do things or know things without her ever saying a word to me." He paused, eyeing his shot. "It's like I'm supposed to know what she's thinking."

Ethan smiled, "Must be rough figuring all of that out."

Johnny nodded. "Sometimes it is." He softened his tone, "We're just so different."

"I know and I thought that's what made you two work so good together."

"Yeah, but it gets in the way too." Johnny missed his shot. "It seems like I'm always wanting to go out and do stuff, you know, be with friends, family, and other couples. She wants to stay at home, work on the house, lounge around, and do I don't know what."

"She's not always like that though." Ethan said as he watched Johnny shoot. "Brooke likes to get out, play games, go to dinners and parties. She's funny too."

Johnny peered at the pool table as though he was seeing straight through it. "Sometimes I just wonder."

"Wonder what?"

"If we made the right choice."

Ethan walked over to him, glaring. "You know you did. What are you talking about?"

"Don't get me wrong. I love Brooke with all my heart, she's amazing." He paused, "But sometimes I just wonder if I would have worked better with someone else or if she would have been happier with someone who was more like her."

"Eight ball, corner pocket," proclaimed Ethan.

"I don't know what I'm talking about," said Johnny as he exhaled.

After Ethan sank the shot he said, "No, you don't know what you're talking about." He looked at Johnny square in the eyes. "Your turn to rack 'em."

After Ethan began the next game of pool he chalked the end of his cue stick and looked toward the bar. Melinda and Elizabeth were still there.

"You should enjoy your single life while you can," said Johnny.

"I've heard that one before."

"Think about it, you have no responsibilities other than to yourself. You can come and go as you please."

"That's true, but that's the only good thing about being single. You know I wish I was in your shoes."

"I know you do. But do something for me, date around, meet some new women." Johnny glanced at the bar. "Go talk to one of those two."

"Why? I already like Amy."

Johnny rolled his eyes. "But you're not defined, you're not tied to anything yet."

Ethan didn't say anything.

"You've got to wake up. There are plenty of options right in front of you."

Ethan was picky. His friends thought he was anyway. The truth was, he saw what his parents had, and knew that's what he wanted. He saw the way his parents smothered each other with random kisses, tiny surprises, and how they were always supportive of one another. They were in love. He wasn't willing to settle for anything less, than what he saw love was supposed to be like. Ethan claimed he'd somehow *know it* when he'd found the right person.

Ethan cleared his throat. "I don't care what you think." He put the bottom of his pool stick on the ground. "I know what I'm looking for." He cleared his throat. "And I might have actually found it with Amy." Ethan grinned.

Johnny shook his head from side to side. "Well, I hope so, but I guess we'll see."

CHAPTER 17

Jeanne emerged from the kitchen, hidden by a cloud of steam. She carried a plate of corn on the cob, just pulled from a pot of boiling water. Since Amy was joining the family for dinner tonight, Jeanne couldn't resist making Ethan's favorite. Green bean casserole, applesauce, pickles, and chicken David had grilled outside only minutes ago, covered the table.

When Jeanne suggested to Ethan that he invite Amy over for dinner Saturday night, he thought, *why not*. They'd talked on the phone everyday while she was vacationing and when he mentioned the idea of dinner to her she sounded as though she'd be up for it. Amy had gotten back to Indiana earlier that same morning.

After everyone found their seats around the table, David folded his hands, bowed his head, and prayed. It was something their family had always deemed important and they hadn't gone a meal without. As soon as the prayer ended Jeanne reached for her glass of water, took a drink, then left the table to get something she'd forgotten in the kitchen.

Ethan looked at his father. "So what did she forget this time?" he asked. Ethan explained to Amy how this could be counted on for each meal. Whether it was the salt and pepper, a side dish, or napkins, there was always some reason that Jeanne had to get up from the table. Ethan and David figured it was the consummate host in Jeanne and a little bit of her perfectionism shining through too.

Jeanne, always full of questions and a great conversationalist, asked Amy all sorts of questions throughout dinner. One of Jeanne's questions was about her trip. "So how was Florida?"

Amy told the story of how she'd been parasailing. She loved floating in mid air, nearly as high as the hotels that lined the beach. It wasn't as breezy as she imagined and the harness wasn't that uncomfortable. Yet, just one day after she'd gone she read an article in the local newspaper about someone's harness coming loose doing that very same thing. Luckily, there was a person on the beach who noticed something was wrong so they grabbed the rope dangling hundreds of feet below the person, and wrestled them to safety. If she had read that article beforehand, then she probably would not have gone.

Amy also spoke of how she decided to become a teacher, which made Jeanne's face glow with approval. During her first year of teaching, all of the students had been great to work with, but one. She had a little boy always harassing her, making fun of her lessons, as well as the other kids. Day after day, she made him sit in the corner or miss recess. That was rough for her to deal with, but she worked her way through it.

She told them about the school play she was helping to organize. Three weeks ago, her principal cornered her and asked her if she'd direct "The Lewis and Clark Adventures." She really didn't want to. She ended up agreeing to assistant the director. Now, two months of her life were already planned for her. Between after-school practice, set construction, and coming up with wardrobes, her to do list was overwhelming.

"What a coincidence," said Jeanne. "Did you know Ethan was once an actor?"

Ethan dropped onto his plate the spoon full of applesauce he was about to devour. He exhaled, then smiled and shook his head.

Amy could tell that there must be a story

involved. "Do tell," she said.

David grinned along with Ethan as Jeanne began.

"It must have been, what, fourth grade?"

"That sounds right," said David.

"Our little aspiring actor was Clark, in 'The Lewis and Clark Adventures.'" She poured herself another glass of water from the pitcher, then offered it to everyone else. They all nodded that they were fine. "It was the end of the year school play and the entire gymnasium was packed full of people. Every seat in the bleachers was filled, and there were folding chairs all over the basketball court too." She grinned. "Everyone was there."

"It was some performance, wasn't it, Mother?" asked Ethan.

"I doubt if anyone has been able to forget it."

Amy nodded as though impressed, yet she knew that she didn't have the entire story.

"Our little Ethan was sitting on one of those black, plastic chairs with a seat that looks like a snow shovel. Do you know what I mean?" asked Jeanne.

"Of course, that's what we have at our school too."

"Anyway, the poor thing was a nervous wreck beforehand, so I told him just to give it his best and just have fun." Jeanne sipped water. "Well, when Ethan stood up to chime in with his very first line, everyone in the audience started laughing."

Ethan wide-eyed his mother. "All right, I'll take it from here," he said. He shifted in his seat. "I was so nervous. My palms were sweating, my neck was itchy, I couldn't remember my lines, and I had to go to the bathroom so bad that I couldn't hold it."

Amy's mouth fell open.

"Yep, I peed my pants," he said.

Amy reached for his shoulder as though to comfort him all these years later. Then all of them began to chuckle out loud.

Ethan continued, "Everyone knew it too. I had a huge wet ring in my blue jeans." He glanced at his plate of half eaten food. "The worst part of it all was that I had to walk around on that stage in front of everyone in my own urinated blue jeans for an hour."

"But, he did nail all of his lines," added David.

"You'll never guess what my nickname was after that?"

Amy shook her head. "What?"

"Squirt."

Amy giggled. "Really?"

Ethan laughed, while nodding.

Amy grinned at Ethan. "Any other stories like this that I need to know about?" she asked.

David perked up.

"I can think of one that's pretty good."

"Oh great," said Ethan. "Why don't we just see if we can completely embarrass Ethan?"

"That last story was so cute," said Amy. "How

about just one more?"

Ethan smirked, "All right, but this is it dad."

David swallowed. "Ethan has a cousin that is big-time into cowboy stuff. He's lassoed calves, ridden bulls, and trained hundreds of horses."

"I had an uncle that did that too," she said.

David took a quick sip of water. "Have you ever seen the show 'The Lone Ranger?'"

"I can't say that I have."

"Well it's about a cowboy, some Indians, and a lot of fights and horse chases. Anyway, my uncle had a horse named Daisy, and he asked if we would take care of her for one summer, so we did. One day those two boys, when they were about twelve-years-old, decided they were going to try and ride that horse bareback, meaning without a saddle." Amy's eyebrows rose. "Not only that, they were trying to run up behind her, jump on, and go, all in one motion."

Ethan grinned and nodded.

David continued, "What's funny is, I remember doing that very same thing when I was about that age too. The Lone Ranger rode that way all the time. Anyway, when Ethan went to jump up on her, he didn't quite make it over her rump. He got stuck on the very top part of her rear. To keep his balance he squeezed his legs together. When he did that he must have pressed against a sensitive area or something because she freaked out. That horse bucked him off and kicked him in the groin in mid-air."

Amy's eyes widened and she exhaled as though she were in pain.

Ethan nodded his head. "Thanks, for telling that one."

David smiled. "It was the least I could do."

"I was stuck sitting in that very chair right over there." He pointed into the living room at a well-worn, dark blue recliner. "I had to ice things down for two full days." He grinned.

Jeanne looked at Amy as though they had some sort of secret understanding of what each other was thinking. "Boys will be boys."

"I guess that's the truth," said Amy.

The rest of the dinner progressed in much the same way. David and Jeanne took turns revealing little tidbits about Ethan through a few more childhood stories. Amy seemed to enjoy each one of them.

After the dinner table had been cleared, the four of them were taking their first bite of pecan pie when Amy asked a question. "So how did you two meet?"

Jeanne glanced toward David, smiling. "We were high school sweethearts."

"Aw," said Amy.

David chimed in, "We've actually known each other since childhood. We have a black and white photo of us as children standing beside each other that her mother took."

"Our families went to the same church when we

were growing up," added Jeanne.

"That's so neat." Amy savored a bite of the pie and then began again. "Who asked who out? If I may ask?"

"No problem at all," said Jeanne. "David asked me to prom when we were juniors and we've been together ever since."

"And how long has that been?"

"This year will be our fortieth anniversary." Jeanne gushed, peering at David.

"That is so precious." Amy gleamed. "You two are rare."

"How's that?" asked Jeanne.

"A marriage that has lasted forty years. That's incredible."

"It is, isn't it?" stated David.

They all sat in agreement, enjoying the last few bites of their pie. Once they were all finished, Jeanne brought a freshly brewed pot of coffee to the table, offering it to everyone. That gesture had become a trademark of theirs. They always had coffee at the table after dessert. Once everyone was satisfied and had prepped their coffee to their liking, Amy leaned forward on the table.

"Can I ask another sort of personal question?"

Jeanne and David, whom she was looking at, shrugged their shoulders.

"How did you guys know?"

"Know what?" asked Jeanne.

"That you were meant to be together."

Ethan was surprised she was so comfortable with his parents. *Must be a good thing.*

Jeanne and David looked at each other as if asking, *Do you want to take this one?*

"I always had a thing for him, even when we were growing up." Jeanne smiled. "Well, I knew he was a sweetheart, came from a great family, and would treat me right. I knew his heart, that he had a great work ethic, and that he could dream." Jeanne's eyes suddenly became shiny. "That's the man I fell in love with almost forty years ago." She blushed. "And that's the man I'm still in love with today."

David swallowed another drink of coffee, then cleared his throat.

"I would say the same thing." He set his coffee down. "By the time we got married, we knew so much about each other that I had no doubts whatsoever. She's the only girlfriend I ever had, and I wouldn't have it any other way."

Jeanne glanced at David, almost as though asking for permission. Jeanne found Amy's eyes again. "I'll tell you when I really knew," she said softly. "The night of those tornadoes, the ones from 1965." She continued, "My father and I went to David's farm to find him, but he wasn't there. No one was. It was that night that I knew I was in love with David, and that I wanted to be with him for the rest of my life."

"Which reminds me, Amy," David said as he

found her eyes. "I want to thank you for inviting Ethan to meet your grandmother. If you wouldn't have, then I probably never would have seen my father's journal." He glanced at his brown mug, which he was cupping with his hands. "Thank you."

"I'm just glad you were able to find something."

David agreed. "I feel like I've learned more about my father through that journal than I ever did growing up." He clenched his jaw. "It makes me miss him," he said softly.

Once the heavy air cleared from the dinner table a silence fell between all of them. Ethan had been wrestling with bringing something up.

"Dad, did you ever read that book her grandpa wrote?"

David stiffened. He cleared his throat. "Parts of it."

Ethan looked at his mother and Amy. "Did either of you?" he asked. They both nodded, yes.

"Wasn't the part about that little girl one of the saddest things you've ever heard?" he asked.

David met Ethan's eyes, exhaled, then clenched his empty coffee mug, drained of every last drop. He was drained too. David was tired of reliving the past Ethan kept bringing to life.

David stood up, pushed his chair in, and walked away.

CHAPTER 18

Shivers traveled up and down David's spine when he realized where he was - on all fours, hovering over Rebecca. His elbows were screaming at him in pain because tiny little pebbles of dirt had carved their way into his skin. The cement walls surrounding him began to blend together. He was about to faint. He fought the nausea building in his gut. David breathed heavy and looked underneath his torso to make sure that he'd protected Rebecca from the whistling winds above them.

Rebecca wasn't there.

His pulse raced into double time and he felt

moist on his forehead and under his arms. His eyes searched the gray walls for Rebecca's bouncing blonde curls, but he saw nothing. He called out her name, over and over, screaming louder each time.

"Rebecca!"

"Rebecca, it's okay, I'm right here."

"Where are you?"

"Rebecca!"

He knew he didn't have the strength to stand, so he began crawling. He guessed she might have gotten scared and crawled to a corner or was hiding beneath something. Debris flew at him from all directions. He couldn't tell what anything was or where he was going.

"Rebecca!"

The more he crawled, the weaker he felt, yet something in him would not give up. He kept crawling, feeling the grit of loose dirt and the scrape of raw cement scuffing at his fingers. His knuckles began to bleed, his head bobbed, and his lungs felt empty. Finally, he collapsed, sprawling his arms out.

To his surprise, he saw nothing but a clear blue sky above him. All of the rain had passed. The wind stopped. The dark clouds vanished. Then the sun warmed his face.

As he lay there, he could feel liquid sliding down the side of his cheek and around his ear. He tried to lift his right hand to find the source, but it felt as though there were a fifty-pound dumbbell attached to it. Even without touching his head, he knew he was bleeding. He didn't feel any pain, just the steady ooze. That's when he noticed how heavy his chest felt, expanding and contracting as though someone were sitting on top of him.

A puddle formed underneath his neck, moistening his back. Strangely, he began to see things around him more clearly. Green beans and peaches were scattered everywhere, glass from their containers made a carpet on the basement floor. The cabinet they had been sitting on was leaning against the wall at a forty-five degree angle. Broken pieces of wood had been tossed around as though part of a game of pick-up sticks.

Examining the wall in front of him he saw that the very stairs he'd run down only moments earlier were now gone. That's when he remembered, so was Rebecca. His eyes searched, scanning the corners of the basement, but no one was down there except him.

A tear slithered its way out of the corner of his eye until it landed in the outer rim of his earlobe. He wanted to get up so badly, but he couldn't.

Everything went black.

When he opened his eyes, he was curled up in bed, facing Jeanne. She had been watching him.

Jeanne had been experiencing David's dream season for years. At first, she got frightened because she said she never knew what he was going to do. But eventually, she grew used to it.

David's reactions to his dreams were rarely the same. He found solace knowing Jeanne would always be there to comfort him.

She wiped a tear from the crest of his cheekbone. "I love you," she said.

CHAPTER 19

"I was making a fort out of fallen branches and old logs over there underneath that oak tree," David said as he pointed toward the base of the tree. "I used to do things like that all the time, but especially after a fight with my parents."

Ethan and his father were standing less than twenty-five yards from a creek that twisted like a pretzel, weaving in and out as though there were two streams. Ethan could only imagine what his father had gone through, and was going through on a day like today. Today was Palm Sunday, forty years to the day.

"You had a fight?" asked Ethan.

David took a few more steps toward the tree whose branches were stretched far, as though trying to grab the sky. Fresh green leaves ruffled against each other.

"We sure did and I caused it all to happen." David peered up and down the creek.

Ethan looked too, taking in the vast array of wild green grass, weeds, and flower blossoms surrounding them. It was as though that river had all of the answers running through it.

"I had just turned eighteen and thought I could tell my parents what to do." He grinned as he shook his head from side to side. A gentle breeze ran through his hair, parting it to the left. "I didn't want to go to church and I made sure my father knew it. So, he and I yelled at each other a little bit."

David looked down at his feet and put his hands in his pockets. "We had a fight and that's the last memory I've carried with me all these years." He looked up at Ethan. "Well, one of them."

Ethan knew it wasn't his place to ask questions. His father was going to tell him everything; that's why they were here.

"I can still see it all like it was yesterday," David continued. "The clouds came in from over there as fast as I've ever seen clouds move." He pointed toward the southwest at a tan house. "That farm over there used to be my uncle's. When I saw those clouds I watched for a little bit and noticed how calm everything seemed. The next thing I knew, the winds started racing through the leaves, the skies got darker, and the water in the river was choppy. As soon as I saw my uncle's trees bending over, I ran to the house."

David began walking away from the creek, so Ethan followed him. David exhaled. "It was just a few hundred yards to the front door, but by the time I got there, all of the clouds were directly above me."

A few moments later, the two of them were standing in the middle of what had become a cow pasture. "This is close to where the front door was." David acted as though he'd opened the door and let himself in. "My mother was standing over there, in the kitchen. I ran to her first." He walked past a patch of cloves to a barren spot of dirt. "The stairway to upstairs was right here. I ran up to get my father, who was sleeping. I woke him up and we both looked out the window. I'll never forget what I saw." David gazed out over the field. "There were two tornadoes heading straight toward the house, one right after the other. My father yelled for all of us to get to the basement."

Then David found Ethan's eyes, looking into them as though he'd committed a great sin. "Ethan," he swallowed, "I have to tell you something that I should have told you a long time ago." David glanced at the ground, kicked a stone, and then looked back at Ethan. "I have never known quite how to do this." He drew in a long breath. "I had a sister."

Ethan froze. "A sister?" he asked in a whisper of disbelief.

David nodded. "Her name was Rebecca. She was two years old."

Ethan didn't say anything.

David took three hurdle strides in front of him and turned to his left. "This is where she was," he said. Then he paused as though he could depict the exact scene right in front of him. "She was on the floor playing with two teddy bears. Her innocent eyes looked at me as I grabbed her and ran to the basement." He hesitated, "You know that teddy bear I pulled out of that trunk?"

Ethan nodded.

"That's what Rebecca was holding as we ran downstairs."

Ethan raised his eyebrows.

David took a step back, "My father swung open the basement door as I ran down holding Rebecca." He looked up at Ethan. "It was so windy that I could barely keep on my feet. Two-by-fours were snapping all around me."

David wiped his face with his hands. "The stairs underneath me were being sucked up into the air. The jolt of them coming loose sent me falling forward. Since I was holding Rebecca, I turned in mid-air to land on my back so I wouldn't smash her." David imitated rolling on his back as he headed toward the ground. "I needed to land like this."

David turned away from Ethan. "That's when I saw my parents for the last time. They were holding each other. The wind took the stairway right out of the basement and my parents were carried away along with it." David wiped his eyes. "The next thing I knew, I was in a bed at General Hospital."

Ethan's lips parted.

"Apparently, I cracked my head pretty hard on the cement floor." David rubbed the back of his head. "I can't remember anything, but the doctors said I most likely knocked myself out." He gazed at the rolling corn and bean fields around them.

David held out his hands, analyzing his palms. "I failed," he whispered.

He wiped his face with his hands as though trying to wipe away his emotions. He cleared his throat. "No one really knows what happened to Rebecca. I think it was that second tornado. Somehow it managed to pull her out of my arms." He paused, "I know I shouldn't blame myself, but what if I would have run faster, left the tree earlier, not yelled at my dad, or just held onto Rebecca." He caught his breath, "Then maybe everything would be different."

David turned his back from Ethan, started walking toward the river, and then stopped. He came back toward Ethan, clenching his jaw.

"You know that book Amy's grandfather

wrote?" asked David.

Ethan nodded.

"The story about the little girl," David paused. "The one that rips your heart out." He glared at Ethan. "That was about Rebecca." He knelt down, picked up a stone, and threw it. "That story was printed without my blessing. That's why I have a problem with that whole family."

Ethan put his hands in his jean pockets. "Dad, I'm sorry." He paused, "I didn't know."

"I know you didn't." David wiped his hands free of the dust. "I'm sorry I couldn't bring myself to tell you this sooner."

Ethan didn't reply. That was the wall, the unspoken reason, David had let come between them.

David knelt down and brushed dirt away as though he was an archeologist. He uncovered the edges of a cement block.

"I shouldn't have sold this land." David muttered, shaking his head. "A farmer made an offer on it about two weeks after those tornadoes came through." David pressed his lips together. "Man, I can't believe I did that. It just seemed like the right thing to do at the time." He smirked. "You know, instead of rebuilding the house they just filled the basement with dirt, almost as though someone wanted to pretend the house was never here." David glanced at Ethan. "Now, it's just part of a pasture."

Ethan stood in silence.

David grabbed a handful of loose dirt and sifted

it through his fingers. "I never got to see my parents again," he said matter of fact. "No one would let me look at them after the tornado. The doctors said their bodies weren't something I wanted to have as a picture in my mind." He exhaled sharply, releasing years of secrets. "You know those shoes we got out of that trunk?" He looked at Ethan for an understanding nod. "Those were the ones my mother was wearing that day."

David knelt down and grabbed another handful of dirt, "They found my parents about a mile that way." He pointed toward the neighbor's house, and then moved beside Ethan.

"I wish I knew exactly what happened to Rebecca." He tossed a pebble to the ground. "I guess, at least I know she is with mom and dad. I saw it with my own eyes." He hesitated. "I still can't get that image out of my mind." He glanced at Ethan. "My family was part of a mass service in an old high school gymnasium. There was a line of caskets of people who were killed by those tornadoes. I don't even know how many there were. That whole day is such a blur."

He knelt down and grabbed another handful of dirt, sifting it through his fingers. "Anyway, you know that diary we found?" he asked. "I saw your grandfather writing in it that afternoon."

David clenched his jaw. "I can't believe those Yoders kept those things from me." He pleaded to Ethan, looking for affirmation.

Ethan took his hands out of his pockets. "Dad, how do you know they didn't try to give those things to you a long time ago?" He tilted his head. "You haven't exactly been the friendliest toward them."

David glared at Ethan. "When I was released from the hospital, teams of people had already come out here and picked up most of the debris. I'm sure that is when Amy's grandparents found those things and packed them away." David pressed his lips together. "The least they could have done was brought those things to me."

Ethan glanced at his father. "Dad, you're right. But, how do you know they didn't try?"

David smirked. "It wouldn't have taken that much effort to find me." He looked down at the ground. "I was in the hospital for three days. I had more people stop by to check on me than I knew what to do with." David's voice hardened.

David clenched his jaw. "Amy's grandfather was the one who told me that my parents were dead."

CHAPTER 20

Ethan and Amy hadn't talked much lately. She hadn't come to One More Cup at all. Ethan couldn't figure out what he'd done wrong. There were so many things right about Amy that he had to find out what had happened between them.

Ethan tried calling her three times, but she never picked up. He'd left her one voicemail. *Men's Health* said he'd be wasting his time if he tried to pursue a woman who wasn't interested. *How could that be? They were perfect for each other. Things seemed to click.* At least that's what Ethan thought.

When they finally did talk on the telephone Amy

sounded as sweet as she had all those times before, as though they were close friends again. She joked around playfully and seemed more than happy to meet Ethan at Raider Field when he'd suggested it. Raider Field was Ethan's high school baseball field. It was situated in the back corner of the school property, where few cars ever ventured at night.

After Ethan hurled himself over the fence, he looked toward the bleachers and saw Amy sprawled out with her head pointed toward the sky.

He took his time approaching the bleachers. "Some night, isn't it," he said.

Amy glanced at him. "It sure is."

She sat up as he climbed the bleachers. After they'd hugged, Ethan asked her how school had been going. She explained how she had to break up a tussle and make two boys stand in opposite corners facing the wall for the entire hour of recess.

Ironically, that's exactly how Ethan felt he and Amy had been lately.

Then she told him that she'd be taking more courses at IUSB to get her Master's degree and that her schedule was getting too busy.

When Amy asked Ethan if he had started his job search yet, he grinned and said yes. He explained how an acquaintance of Johnny had offered him an engineering position. He was still thinking it through, but was leaning toward taking the job. She laughed when he said he missed his old salary.

Once the small talk was through, the two of

them leaned their backs against the row behind
them. They admired the speckles of glitter scattered
across the black canvas above.

"Do you think that's a planet over there by the
moon," Amy asked. She knew Ethan loved the stars
and most likely would have noticed that one in
particular.

"I was just thinking that same thing," he said. "I
wouldn't put money on it, but I'd guess it's Venus
because I know Mars is over there." He pointed
toward the edge of the Big Dipper.

A soft breeze started to push through the trees on
the other side of the fence slapping leaves against
each other, helping the lull in conversation not seem
quite so long.

Ethan's stomach churned. He had to bring it up.
It was the whole point of seeing her tonight. He
started bouncing his legs up and down quickly
without knowing it. He wished more than anything
that he didn't have to have this conversation. The
back of his neck became itchy. His heart ached. He
cleared his throat.

"Obviously, I can tell things have changed," he
began. "I just want to know what's going on." Like
a bull rider gathering his courage before he set loose
in the ring, Ethan swallowed. "What happened
to…us?"

He waited for her to say something, but nothing
came out of her mouth.

"Did I do or say something wrong?" he asked.

Amy breathed deep. She switched her feet around. "You didn't do anything wrong. You have been wonderful to me."

"Then what's going on?" he asked.

Amy watched the sky, searching for the right words. "I don't know how to explain this."

"Explain what?" Ethan grabbed the back of his neck, rubbing it. He dropped his fisted hand on his thigh, giving himself a slight Charlie-horse.

She exhaled heavily. "Ethan, it's just not there."

He could have predicted something close to those words, but his heart still felt broken into tiny pieces of glass.

Amy sat straight up, glancing at his sunken eyes. "You know how sometimes when you're with someone you have that spark, that little feeling that there's something you can't explain going on?"

She waited for a nod of understanding, but didn't get one. "It's not there for me."

This felt even worse than Ethan imagined.

"Don't get me wrong, Ethan." She put her hand on his shoulder, suddenly consoling him. "I think you are an amazing man and you have such a great heart." Amy paused, "I just don't see us being more than friends. Besides, there's so much history between our families."

Ethan's head jerked toward Amy. "What does that have to do with anything?"

Amy shook her head. "Nothing really."

None of what she just said made sense to him. He wanted to convince her that they just needed to spend more time together to really get to know each other. He loved the way she touched him, how her hair sometimes got caught in her eyelashes, and the way her cheeks got red when she laughed. She hadn't given him any reasons for any of this.

"I don't know what to say. I think you're either hiding something or running away." He exhaled heavily. "Can't we give it a little more time?"

Amy closed her eyes. He knew immediately, he was wasting his time. Her mind was made up.

"I see things so different than you." Ethan's voice was stronger than he thought it would be. "I like us and I want to see if there's something more there."

Amy rested on her elbows, which were situated just behind her. She didn't have anything to say.

Ethan could see she was done with the conversation. A gust of wind blew against them. His shambled heart blew away with it. He felt empty and alone.

Instead of starting a wrestling war with words, he simply looked at her. "I guess the old saying is true," he said, his voice deflated.

She glanced up at him, looking at his dimples. "What's that?"

"Some people come into your life for a season." He paused. "And some for a reason."

She tossed her head back. "Yeah, that makes me

feel real good."

"I think it's true. As bad as I want to see what could be there between us, I know there's nothing I can say that will change your mind. I met you at exactly the right time." He stared at the trees waving back and forth. "If you would have never invited me over to your grandmother's house, I wonder if that trunk would have ever been opened." He glanced back at her. "I doubt that my dad would have ever seen that diary or those shoes."

She looked up at him again. "I'm glad you found it too."

Amy kissed Ethan on the cheek as they hugged good-bye. The gesture seemed to be more apologetic than anything. After she'd left, Ethan sprawled out on the bleachers in the same way she had been when he first got there. The aluminum bleachers that ran down his spine to his legs were cold, but he didn't care. He just wanted to be alone.

CHAPTER 21

Amy sang the words to "Amazing Grace" acapella in front of a crowd of hundreds. It seemed as though the entire community of Middlebury, and a few surrounding towns, had all come to Loucks Cemetery to pay their respects. Many of those who passed away in the tornadoes had been buried at Loucks.

Thick gray clouds smothered the sky. Umbrellas were everywhere echoing the same sound of steady rain. Some people cried, but most had long, weathered faces. Everyone gathered had been affected in one way or another by that fateful day in

1965.

Pastor Hostetler of Forks Mennonite Church gave a short message conveying the hope and peace of God's love. He briefly described the impact of the event on the community. It brought residents closer together. People went out of their way to lend a hand in any way they could, especially to help renovate buildings and offer food to victims. Help came from all over, from the east coast to the west coast, doing whatever was needed. He spoke of how amazing the local police and fire departments were and how the National Guard was there within twenty-four hours. He said these people showed God's love. He remembered the President had recognized the day by visiting the area and declaring special funding to cover some of the millions of dollars in damage. Then he said something that sent shivers up and down Ethan's spine.

"A tornado has no direction, no clear path. Its only purpose is to eliminate anything standing in its way. Though The Palm Sunday Tornado physically succeeded in doing just that, there was one thing that it couldn't take. It couldn't take the heart of this community. All of you know what it means to love your neighbor as yourself. Most people across our country won't remember anything about April 11, 1965, a day that happened so many years ago. There aren't any monuments or special days set aside to mark this tragedy. But we will never forget The Palm Sunday Tornado. Today we are here to honor every single person whose life was taken and send our deepest love to those affected."

The pastor described the path of the tornado outbreak, how the storms traveled from Iowa, to Wisconsin, then south of Chicago, before hitting the open range of Indiana, Michigan, and Ohio. He named all 256 people killed, shared his condolences, and offered a moment of silence.

Florence stepped in front of the crowd, cupping her hands together. She told them about the trunk she'd had in her attic. She'd brought all of the items in the trunk of her car and invited everyone to look through it. With her head bowed, she said, "I did not mean to keep these things from you. I didn't know I had them. From the depths of my heart, please, forgive me."

Amy's song ended the short service. As she sang, Ethan saw his father wiping his eyes. Jeanne had wrapped her arm around his waist and pulled him close. He thought about something his father had said earlier that morning. "Your mother has never left my side. She sat with me in the hospital, went with me when I first saw what used to be my house, and has kissed me goodnight every night since."

After the song ended, his father and mother shook hands and received condolences from people who knew their story. Ethan saw Amy, but received only a quick smile as she left with her parents. He knew better than to expect anything more.

David grabbed Ethan by the hand. "Come on," he said.

David, Jeanne, and Ethan walked together toward a gray marble headstone that read Miller on it. Ethan had never seen it before. Jeanne had brought a few daisies with her. She knelt down quickly planting the three flowers in front of the headstone. They were yellow and stood tall.

The headstone read, "The Millers, A lifetime of Love." Directly beside it was a second stone, the size of a book cover, sticking straight out of the ground. It read, "Rebecca, A giver of endless love." Ethan reached his hand out and rested it on top of the stone feeling both the gritty and smooth edges.

David and Jeanne held each other tightly and asked Ethan to join them as they closed their eyes and said a prayer together.

When they were leaving, Ethan walked a step behind. His parents were holding hands. They gave a few head nods, but neither of them spoke to anyone. As David opened the car door for Jeanne, Ethan remembered the very last words his father said to him when they were standing at the base of what would have been his home.

"Your mother is the only thing that's ever turned out right for me."

CHAPTER 22

David's eyes were staring directly into the familiar blue ones he'd been searching for. It was Rebecca. His hands were on her shoulders as he knelt in front of her. They were on the ledge of the foundation of his house. To his right, was the basement, cluttered with shattered glass and broken wood. He noticed a pile of blood where the bottom of the stairway would have been.

He tried to utter a word, but he couldn't get anything out. He needed the air in his lungs for each gasp of breathe. She tilted her head and smiled at him. David glanced at his left hand, which cupped her teddy bear. He held it up, offering it to her. She grabbed it and jumped into his arms. David closed his eyes as he embraced Rebecca. When he opened them, his parents were standing behind her, holding hands. All of their clothes were clean, just as they had been before the tornado came through. None of them said anything; they simply smiled and looked at him.

Rebecca tried to hand the teddy bear back to David. He tilted his head and wrinkled his forehead, confused.

"Take it," she said playfully. "I want you to have him."

David reluctantly took hold of it, just as Rebecca stepped backward. He tried to get up, but he couldn't. He had lost control of his arms and legs. He was frozen, kneeling at eye-level to Rebecca.

"Davey," said the soft voice of Rebecca. "I'm okay." She looked up at her parents. "I'm with mommy and daddy."

David closed his eyes as tears began to stream down his cheeks.

"Son, we're all okay," said a deep, comforting voice. David knew it was his father. "We love you, and we are so proud of you."

Then, everything went black. He fought to see through the dark fog, but he couldn't see anything.

The next time he could make anything out, he was lying in bed, looking straight up at the ceiling. He tried to fall asleep right away, hoping to go back to that dream. When he realized he couldn't, he rolled toward his wife. She stirred and then looked at him seeing his eyes on her. He smiled.

"Honey?"

David exhaled in relief. "Everyone's okay," he whispered.

Just by the look on his face, she knew what he was talking about. "I know they are," she said.

David leaned toward Jeanne, and then kissed her on the lips.

CHAPTER 23

"This is it," Ethan announced.

David sat down beside his son. They were on the bank of the St. Joseph River; Ethan had taken his father to the place he and Johnny had come so many times. David looked around at the boarded up windows, graffiti spray-painted on the base of The Armory, and the town's river walk on the other side of the river.

The first stars of the night glittered in the dimly lit sky. The faint sound of cars withered in the background giving way to the soothing ripple of the river. They sat, listening.

"So this is a caramel what?" asked David.

"A caramel macchiato." Ethan smiled. "It's basically milk, vanilla and caramel flavoring, and a shot of espresso."

"It's sweet, that's for sure."

"I thought you might think that, but it's one of my favorite drinks."

They had dropped in at One More Cup since David had never been there. Ethan fixed them both a drink. His father browsed the framed art for sale on the walls and glanced through the newspaper. He nodded his head, an approval of some sort, as they were leaving.

"You and Johnny used to come here?"

"Off and on for a few years."

"So this is where you were when you had that Mad Dog 20/20 stuff?" David smirked.

Ethan shook his head. "Sure is."

"I can't believe you thought we would think you were sick." David looked at Ethan. "Your eyes were blood shot and I could smell the alcohol seeping out of your pores."

"I know. I was an idiot."

"At least you learned from it."

"Live and learn, right?"

David didn't say anything. He took a swig of his coffee and stared at the river.

"So how are you doing?" asked David.

Ethan was counting the ripples in the river, waiting for his father to ask. He knew he would.

Over the past couple of days Ethan had been noticeably quiet.

David always knew when Ethan was going through a *time of transition,* as he liked to put it. He said he could sense it.

"I don't know, dad." Ethan picked up a pebble and tossed it into the river. "I just don't get it sometimes." He exhaled, and then took a drink of his coffee. "Whenever I think I can see where my life is heading, it never goes that way. Look at where I am: I'm twenty-six years old, single, and eating at your dinner table."

David looked up at the sky, taking in the Big Dipper directly above them. "You know, your grandpa was one of the greatest men I've ever known."

Ethan glanced at his father. He noticed the wear and tear of a long life stretched across his father's tired face.

"People loved him, his sense of humor, and his relentless smile. He always found a way to smile. It didn't matter how tough of a day he'd had - and he was a hard worker, too - somehow he'd find a smile and he'd give it to someone. He had a way of making each person feel important." David took a swig of his coffee. "I wish you could have met him, you would have liked him."

"I wish I could have too." Ethan brushed his right hand over the top of the freshly cut grass to the right of where he was seated.

"And your grandmother, boy was she a pistol." David chuckled to himself. "She was bound and determined to make a responsible man out of me. One night I was late to dinner because I had to finish feeding our horses. She said to be seated at the table by six. Well, I wasn't. So once I sat down, she took my silverware and plate away and made me watch while they ate."

Ethan laughed.

David looked at Ethan, watching him study the ripples of the river. "I'm sorry," he said.

Ethan turned his head, finding his father's eyes on him. "What?"

"I'm sorry I wasn't as good of a father as I had."

"Dad." Ethan shook his head from side to side. "What are you talking about?"

"No, I'm serious." David clenched his jaw. "I've hid part of my life from you for so long. I didn't mean to, but I didn't want you to feel sorry for me." David pressed his lips together as he searched for the right words. "I didn't want you to know I let Rebecca die."

Ethan glanced at his father, catching him wiping his eyes. "But dad, you didn't."

David looked down at the moisture beginning to collect on the grass. "I've been trying to tell myself that for years. I don't know if I will ever believe that it wasn't my fault. I've always had this little piece of me that believes I failed." David exhaled. "I let my parents down, I let Rebecca down, and I never had a chance to make it right with any of them." David swallowed with difficulty. "I have missed my family so badly."

Ethan set his to-go coffee cup in the grass. "Dad, I can't imagine what you went through. I can't imagine being in the middle of a tornado. I can't imagine my life without mom or you." He looked his father in the eyes. "I wish I could take everything you had to go through and wipe it away."

Ethan reached out his left arm, pulled his father close, and embraced him.

"I'm sorry," said David again.

Ethan hugged him tighter. "Dad, don't be." He sniffed. "You've been a great dad."

The two embraced, listening to the trickle of the river, until they patted each other on the back. David exhaled loudly as though he'd been holding his breath.

Ethan wiped the corners of his eyes. "You know, you and mom have been through a lot together."

David nodded. "We sure have." He watched the ripple of the river, flashing back to the tornado again. "I'm so lucky I had her right when I needed her." He smirked. "Did you know I moved in with her family the day I came home from the hospital?"

Ethan tilted his head. "No, I guess I didn't."

"I knew from that moment on, I would be with her forever," said David. He blinked slowly, remembering that day.

Ethan sniffed. "I look at you and Mom, and I wonder, how in the world am I ever going to find something like that?"

David laughed under his breath.

Ethan tossed a few pebbles to the bottom of the river and looked at his father with a grin. "You two really love each other." Ethan drew in a long breath. "I don't know what that's like, and I wish so badly that I did."

"You will, Ethan. When you meet the right woman, you will."

CHAPTER 24

"Did I get the right ones?"

David asked Ethan to pick up some daisies and roses on his way home from work.

"Perfect." David nodded in appreciation. "She's going to love them." He stood at the stove wearing an apron. "Can you do me one last favor and cut the ends off? Then grab that vase over there on the table and put them in it, along with a little water."

Ethan nodded. "No problem." After he situated the daisies just right, he brought in the roses and set them on the counter. Then he poured himself a glass of water and leaned against the doorway, watching his father. David kept taking deep breaths.

"You holding up okay?" asked Ethan.

David continued slicing mushrooms without much thought. "So far, everything is going according to plan." He grinned, "But there's a long way to go."

Ethan stood there until he finished his water. He and his father joked about past anniversaries. One year Ethan forgot. He tried to make it up to his parents by washing dishes for a week - a nice gesture for a sixteen-year-old. David had always been good at doing something special, but this year was going to top them all.

David's plan was working. Just before lunch, he dropped off a note at school, asking the secretary if she would slide it under Jeanne's door. The secretary smiled after David explained its importance.

Shortly after David left, he'd been feeling antsy, as though he had too much coffee. He wanted everything to go perfect. By the time he got home, he wondered if Jeanne was reading the note...

Happy Anniversary Honey!

I'm going to have to ask a favor of you...I need you to stop by Grayce's Massages for me on your way home from work. Make sure to get there by four o'clock.

Love you ~ David

Jeanne's insides warmed just thinking about what might be in store for tonight. She always looked forward to their anniversary, not just because it marked another year spent together, but also because David never shied from spoiling her with love and affection.

After school was out, Jeanne left the papers to grade sitting on her desk and grabbed her keys. This was her day. That stuff could wait until tomorrow. On one anniversary she and David both took off work and went to Grand Haven, Michigan. They walked around peeking in the antique shops and strolled along the pier to a lighthouse on Lake Michigan. They had gotten pretty good at getting away for a day or two at a nearby town on the lake. It made them feel like they were taking a mini-vacation. She knew that wasn't going to happen this year, but it made no difference to her whether they left or stayed. She was simply happy with her husband and the lifestyle they lived.

When she walked in the door, she announced herself and a young lady, just out of high school, escorted her to a room. Shortly thereafter, a lady in her mid-thirties, with blonde hair pulled back tight against her head, asked Jeanne to slip into the robe folded beside the chair she was sitting on. She wanted Jeanne to make herself comfortable.

Moments later, Jeanne was face down, staring at the floor through an opening in a padded headrest listening to "The Sounds of Water" as the masseuse rubbed lilac scented oil into her back.

An hour later, Jeanne's body felt utterly relaxed. She was worn out and refreshed at the same time. After the masseuse left, her original escort, grabbed her by the arm and led her to the room next door, empty save for a leather padded salon chair. She was given a manicure and a pedicure, then a stylist appeared from nowhere and made up her hair and make up. She was escorted back into the massage room to get dressed. There was a black cocktail dress hanging from a hook along the wall.

The young lady pointed to the dress. "This is for you," she said. Underneath it was a pair of black dress shoes.

Jeanne gushed. She slipped into the dress, which fit perfectly. As she closed the door behind her, the young lady escorted her out the front door, where a young gentleman in a black suit and yellow tie was standing. It was Ethan.

"Mrs. Miller, your ride awaits you." He smiled.

Jeanne thanked the young lady for everything, taking Ethan's arm. He walked her to the passenger side back door of the Honda Accord. He held it open, then let her slide in, and closed it. It was Jeanne's car.

David had dropped Ethan off at Grayce's Massages after the receptionist called to let him know Jeanne was there. His plan was working well, so far.

Jeanne was glowing as she sat in the back seat. She knew better than to try to ask questions and get ideas from Ethan as to what might be happening next. Besides, she loved surprises.

"You look beautiful, Mrs. Miller," Ethan said, making eye contact with her in the rearview mirror.

"Thank you." She glanced out the window at the trees passing by, and then back at Ethan. "By the way, thank you for the necklace," she looked down at her fingertips, which were holding a small birthstone. "I love it." Ethan had handed the gift to her as he helped her in the car.

"You're welcome."

The remainder of the drive was rather silent. They made small talk about their days, but they both knew none of that stuff was really important at a time like this. When Ethan finally pulled in the driveway, he saw that the front door was cracked open, which meant everything was ready to go. He opened the car door, helped his mother out, and escorted her to the front door.

He leaned in and hugged her tightly, kissing her on the cheek. "Happy Anniversary, Mom."

"Thank you."

Jeanne turned toward the front door and saw David, smiling. He opened the front door, holding it as she walked through. He closed both of the doors as Ethan drove away.

"You look beautiful, honey," he said.

"Thank you. You look nice and handsome too."
He was wearing a new black suit with a blue tie he
and Ethan had picked out the day before.

They kissed softly.

As Jeanne turned toward the dining room, she
put her hands over her mouth to cover her gasp.
Hundreds of vanilla candles lit the room. Red rose
petals were scattered around the outer edges of the
shiny hardwood floor. In the middle of the room
was an old-fashioned wooden table. It had been in
the attic of their garage for years. The table
originally belonged to Jeanne's mother. David had
refinished it and repaired its two broken legs. On
top of it was a single candle, place settings for two,
and a bouquet of white daisies. There was soft piano
music playing in the background.

"Oh, David." Her lips pressed together.

She leaned in and kissed him.

When he held her chair out for her and gently
pushed her in place, she noticed the china cabinet in
front of her. It was another piece of furniture of her
mother's. David had refinished that as well.

"Your mother wanted you to have that."

She covered her lips with her fingers. As she
was admiring the cabinet and table, David was
getting the meal he'd prepared.

First he brought her a glass of red wine, which
they drank on rare occasions. That was followed by
fresh rolls, then salad, penne pasta, and grilled

chicken. David wasn't the swiftest in the kitchen.
He did the best he could by himself. Jeanne could
have predicted that very meal, in that exact order,
that's why it was perfect.

Throughout the meal they talked about early
memories. They spoke of when they lived in a
trailer on her parents' land, how they moved to
South Carolina and spent two years in a condo, and
then the day they bought this house.

"Do you ever wish we could have had more
kids?" asked Jeanne. She set her fork down on her
plate and grabbed her wine glass.

David folded his napkin and placed it on top of
his plate. "I've wondered what that would have
been like."

"Me too."

"I don't think I could have handled a daughter
though," he said with a chuckle.

"No? Why not?"

"Eventually she'd turn fifteen or sixteen and
start dating." He exhaled. "I would have never been
able to handle that."

"Why not?"

He slanted his head. "I may be old, but I can
still remember what it was like to be a boy and the
thoughts that ran through my head."

"Boys, boys, boys."

Just then David rose from his seat. He extended
his hand. "Would you dance with me?"

She gleamed up at him. "Absolutely."

Jeanne took his hand and leaned in. She rested her head on his shoulder and swayed back and forth. Standing that close to each other made their hearts beat a step quicker. Every touch seemed brand new. They danced until the CD ran out of songs.

Then they simply stood in the silence of a house that had all of the signs of old age - a leaky faucet, a whistling furnace, and a floor that announced every step that was taken on it.

They kissed softly again, this time more passionately.

"I have one more thing I'd like to give you tonight," David said. "Why don't you have a seat again, while I clear the table and go get it?"

"I can help."

"No, you just sit right there." He showed his hand to the chair. "I'll take care of it and be right back."

Jeanne restarted the CD while David cleared everything away. When he was through, he walked back into the dining room carrying what looked to be a rolled up piece of paper.

He walked to her and knelt down. He held out his hand. In it was a scroll, tightly bound together by a perfectly tied raffia bow.

"What's this?" she asked.

"It's for you. I want you to read it."

She took it from his hand.

David walked out to the kitchen, poured himself another glass of wine, and sat down across the table from Jeanne.

She waited for him to return before she began to untie it. The paper felt gritty and was slightly yellowed as though it was aged. David had taken a page out of his father's diary. The edges had been torn on all four sides. She unraveled the scroll and began to read.

> *To my love,*
> *Why does time never slow down? One minute I'm eighteen with an entire life to live ahead of me and the next I'm wrinkled around my eyes. My back aches every morning when I crawl out of bed. Maybe there's a magic button to push or a specific task I have to do in order to slow this life of mine down. If that's the case, I hope that someone can see that I have no clue what I'm doing and that they need to let me in on the big secret.*
> *We both know that if I could go back and relive any moment of my choice there's one day in particular that I would try to change. The simple fact is there's always going to be a part of me that will feel cheated, as though I was robbed. And no matter what I tell myself, I know that I will always wonder if I might have been responsible in some way or another. I will never forget all that I lost that day.*

Though I never deserved to lose so much, I was also given something that I never could have earned. I have lived a life filled with love. If my one purpose on this earth has been to experience the love you and I share, then my life has been lived to the fullest.

Though you may hide the gray that has crept into your hair and you haven't been happy with your figure ever since you had Ethan, you're still the woman I fell in love with over forty years ago. I love you more today than I ever have.

It's because of you, that I know my life has counted for something. It's because of you, that I can rest knowing my father would be proud of me. It's because of you, that I know what unconditional love means.

I know I haven't made all of your dreams come true and there have been times that I've fallen short of what you might expect of me, but today I have one question that I would like to ask you.

Will you take me as your husband for the next forty years?

David

CHAPTER 25

Late Saturday night, Ethan sipped a cherry
Sprite at One More Cup. The coffee shop was
closed and no one was there but him. He had
worked the evening shift and told his co-worker that
he'd lock up.

Ethan sat at the same table he and Amy had
when they first got to know each other. He had
brought his grandfather's leather diary and had been
making his way through it. After he had finished
reading all of the entries, he was drawn back to one
in particular. He kept reading about how his
grandfather had written a letter to his wife, before

he'd ever met her.

He thought about how upset his father had been that the tradition had ended with him. He also knew that his father then surprised his mother with a similar letter. Ethan decided it was time to follow in those footsteps. He turned to the very last page of the diary and saw the remains of the piece his father had torn out. Ethan grabbed the blank page in front of it and tore it out. He had a feeling his grandfather wouldn't mind.

Ethan found a pen tucked under the counter. In an empty coffee shop, Ethan followed in his father's and grandfather's footsteps, carrying on a family tradition.

At the age of twenty-six, Ethan put the deepest dreams of his heart into words. He wrote a letter to his future wife.

> *If you are reading this, then I am the luckiest man alive. The tides have turned, my karma reversed, because this means that I have fallen in love.*
>
> *As I am writing you this letter, I have no idea who you are, whether we've already met, or if you are waiting for me in the days to come. But as you are reading this, know that it has been written just for you, and that no other eyes will have graced these words before yours.*
>
> *I have thought about you for years. The*

older I get, the more I feel as though I am behind in this life of mine. I'm not sure if there is any way of catching up other than by finding you. I don't expect you to be the answer to all that seems to be missing in my life, but I do believe that there is something amazing, waiting for us to experience together.

I can only imagine what it will feel like to actually give you this letter, realizing that what we have is love. I think that I know what love is, but I can't claim to have been in love yet. My guess is that it will feel something like when I was six years old, when I would tie a red cape around my neck and race through the house in my Superman Underoos. Not only was I invincible, but I'd forget about everything else around me. By me giving you this letter, I'm telling you that this is how you have made me feel.

I'm guessing you have probably had some of the same lonely feelings that I've had along the way. Maybe you know what it's like to have everyone look at you, wondering why you are still single, what you are so picky about, and whether there's something wrong with you? Maybe you've had a day when all you really wanted was for me to wrap my arms around you and tell you that everything was going to be okay.

*Maybe you have compared yourself to your
friends. Most likely, some of them are
married and it seems as though your
timetable in life is so much slower than
theirs. I know those feelings all too well.
Yet even with all of the loneliness that you
and I have been through, every bit of it will
have been worth it to have waited for this
very moment. There is nothing you can do,
nothing you can say, that could make me
love you more. You've already won my
heart completely.*

*I can't help but imagine you as I'm
writing this letter. I wonder what your skin
feels like, the shape your lips take when you
smile, and how much your eyes will tell me
about you. I wonder what it will be like to
trace your face with my fingertips and how
long it will take me to memorize each
feature.*

*I have no idea where your life has taken
you, or what you've been through. But I'm
telling you now, if I haven't already, that I
love you without question, regardless of
where your journey in life has been.*

*I can't promise you that every day will
be exactly how you dreamed it would be.
However, I will never stop my relentless
pursuit to make you smile more than you
ever have before. I will do whatever it takes*

to show you how much I love you.
I am forever yours ~ Ethan

EPILOGUE

Like I said before, I can't imagine being my dad, going through what he did. The pain of his losses must have been unbearable. Even forty years later, I know he still goes back to that day, replaying it. If there was anything I could do for him, or my family, it would be to somehow change that day.

To the many families affected by that Palm Sunday, and any other tornado, my heart goes out to you. Know that I told this story with the greatest of respect to those who lost their lives.

THE STORY BEHIND THE STORY

This all started on December 25, 2003. Yes, I know the exact date. Not just because it was Christmas, but because I was inspired.

I was with my family all day. We had our traditional morning brunch, followed by stockings and presents. I can vividly remember watching my parents. My dad had his arm around my mom. They couldn't stop smiling. They were in the midst of the most important thing to both of them: family. And now that they are grandparents, the importance has multiplied even more.

My parents have been married for over thirty-eight years. Over that time they've certainly had their share of mountains to climb, which, I suppose, is why I sat in awe of them that day.

I had visions of the numerous times our family gathered together around the dining room table. We love to eat, laugh, and tell stories. There are times though when it's tough to smile, such as when my dad talks about his parents being killed on April 11, 1965. It's so hard for me to comprehend that day. I can't imagine being him, experiencing that heartache. I can't imagine being my mom either, standing beside my dad through it all.

After spending Christmas with my family, I went home, sprawled out on my bedroom floor, and began to write. I love to write. I often jot down random thoughts, short stories, or poetry. That night, I found a passion, something that had been inside of me wanting to get out. I started writing everyday, usually after work until my eyes couldn't take it anymore.

The more I wrote, the more I researched that Palm Sunday of 1965. I wanted to know all that happened, what people saw, how they felt, etc. But my motivation for writing this story was not about the destruction of that day. My parents were going to celebrate their anniversary, and I couldn't think of a better gift than to write their story. A story tested and made strong by the events of that day. So, I filled almost every spare moment I had with writing, editing, reading, and writing.

Finally, the day of my parents' anniversary arrived. So, I told my family I needed everyone to meet at mom and dad's house and that I had a surprise. I hadn't let anyone know what I was doing the entire time I wrote the story. I'd managed to keep it a secret. I would have gone nuts if it hadn't been for my wife, Sondra.

I put the novel in a box and wrapped it in red paper. I'll never forget their reaction. My dad pulled out a piece of paper and began reading it out loud. My mom covered her awestruck mouth and my dad's eyes started to tear up. It was wonderful to see how touched they were.

It is with their permission that I am able to offer this story. I will openly admit that I have not told their exact story. I believe that is for them to tell. What I have done is intertwined facts with imagination, and *The Palm Sunday Tornado* is the result.

I hope you've been entertained, that you've learned about April 11, 1965, and that you've been touched by the display of love conveyed.

Visit Timothy Online at
www.TimothyBontrager.com

- Join the eNewsletter
- Share your story
- Submit a review
- Email Timothy
- Refer the book to a friend
- Find out what's next

Contact Timothy by mail at
Timothy Bontrager
P.O. Box 377
Middlebury, IN 46540

MARGARET WARNOCK
6845 FREDERICKSBURG DR. S.
SYLVANIA, OH 43560-3228